# VEGETARIAN MEALS
# IN MINUTES

# VEGETARIAN MEALS IN MINUTES

## Quick to Prepare
## Easy to Cook

## Maggie Black

# W. Foulsham & Co. Ltd.

London • New York • Toronto • Cape Town
Sydney

W. FOULSHAM & COMPANY LIMITED
Yeovil Road, Slough, Berkshire, SL1 4JH

ISBN 0-572-01402-3

Printed in Great Britain, at St. Edmundsbury
Press, Bury St. Edmunds

# CONTENTS

# ACKNOWLEDGMENTS

Both organizations and personal friends have contributed their knowledge, skill and practical help to this book. I want to thank, in particular, John West Foods for both products and information; also Kikkoman Trading Europe and Haldane Foods Ltd, Leicester, for product advice; my greengrocer, Mr K. Malik of Park Fruiterers, Putney, for patiently finding high-quality out-of-season products; the Health Food Counter, Putney for its wide range of health food products and for obtaining others; and the magazine *Healthy Living* for wise advice on many points.

Among personal friends, Pat Knights has brought her long-standing experience as a practical vegetarian to bear on the book as a whole. Yvon Stewart has contributed her sensitive tasting ability and commonsense approach; so has Judy Pointer. I owe a great debt to Gwen Abberley for typing my unseemly manuscript, and not least to my good friend and editor, Wendy Hobson, for her forbearance and help, and for easing both my financial and practical path.

Maggie Black

# INTRODUCTION

It is quite easy to prepare vegetarian (or any other) meals in half an hour if you live on unending fry-ups or raw greens and peanuts. But is it possible to make any reasonably varied meal in around that time? This book proves that the answer is 'Yes!'

*Vegetarian Meals in Minutes* will kill the bogey that vegetable-based meals are dull, and are laborious to cook. It gives busy, everyday people like me the chance to try them if they want to – and that is important because a new slant on cooking can add variety to anyone's diet. Using this book, you can create three-course meals for your family in just 30 minutes – well, a couple may extend to 40!

Of course, you will have to cut some corners and compromise when time is short. It is not difficult to avoid the excesses which modern health experts tilt against in our Western diet – the load of fat, of sugar, of salt, and smooth, fibreless foods we swallow daily. But you will have to limit the range of cooking methods you can use, avoid certain ingredients which take too long to cook, and use at least some processed foods and flavourings. There may be a hundred and one ways to cook potatoes, but not in the time you can give them. But limitations can be a challenge – varying vegetable combinations, using all the available cooking methods, the occasional can or packet, and perhaps a little thinking ahead are simple ways to meet it.

I hope you will find the dishes in the book appealing, varied and tasty. And I can promise my health-conscious friends that the products I have used will do them no harm. I have lived on the dishes made with them while writing this book – and I am in excellent health.

# NOTES ON THE RECIPES

Recipes marked Ⓥ can be used by vegans.

Recipes marked Ⓧ can be left to cook while other parts of the meal are prepared.

All the recipes serve 4 people unless otherwise stated.

Do not mix metric, Imperial and American measures; follow one set of measurement only.

Spoon measurements are level unless otherwise specified, and based on a 5 ml teaspoon and a 15 ml tablespoon.

Eggs are size 3 unless otherwise specified.

# GOOD FOODS TO CHOOSE
## What They Are and Why We Use Them

## Whole-Grain Products

Whole-grain products such as wholemeal (whole wheat) flour and brown rice contain all the nourishment a new plant will need when it grows from the seed. What is good for a plant is good for you and me. Whole-grain products provide us with all a plant's vital nutrients such as protein, vitamins and minerals, and also with fibre for smooth digestion. The proteins in whole-grain foods are especially valuable in vegetarian meals because if these plant proteins are teamed with dried peas, beans or lentils, they give us much the same quality of protein as meat or fish. This is why I have used whole-grain products throughout this book.

## Grains, Nuts and Seeds

Other grains besides wheat and rice have the same value for us. Oats, barley, maize (corn), rye, millet and buckwheat are all valuable foods. So are most nuts and seeds. Peanuts, almonds and Brazil nuts, along with sunflower, pumpkin and sesame seeds are all packed with nourishment; and since they can be bought ready-to-eat, they are ideal for quick vegetarian meal-making. Wholewheat and spinach pasta are also excellent for speedy cooking, particularly if you use the modern, pre-cooked and dried 'instant' pasta which cooks inside 4 minutes or can be left to 'cook itself' with boiling water poured over it.

# Pulses

Pulses, that is dried beans, peas and lentils, contain protein components which are missing in grain proteins but are needed to make them usable by human beings. This is why it makes sense to eat pulses and grains together. Broad beans and bean sprouts can be counted as pulses for this purpose too. So always try to make time to prepare and serve pasta, rice or some type of whole-grain bread with a dish containing beans, peas or sprouts, and vice-versa. However, you do not have to combine them in the same course. If you prefer, you can serve, say, a bean salad as a starter and a dessert containing bread or biscuit crumbs.

The time that most grains and pulses take to cook puts some cooks off trying any vegetarian dishes. However, there are two ways round this problem. First, although fresh vegetables lose food value rapidly when pre-prepared, grains and pulses do not; and since the cooking times, especially of pulses, varies from batch to batch, it makes obvious sense to cook them ahead of time and to chill or freeze them. A wise vegetarian cook, whether she has to work at speed or not, always keeps a stock of cooked brown rice and a small assortment of slow-cooking types of beans in her freezer, ready to reheat. (If freezer space is a problem, it is useful to remember that puréed grains or pulses are excellent for thickening soups or as a base for (fat-free) sauces. They can be puréed in seconds in an electric blender and frozen as purée.)

An even easier way to get some types of cooked beans or chickpeas (garbanzos) is to buy canned ones. Their food value is the same as that of home-cooked ones, and although they are a good deal more expensive than raw, dried beans, they may in fact not cost much more when you take into account the price of gas or electric power.

The cheapest beans (if you grow them yourself) and certainly the quickest to prepare are bean sprouts. They are beautifully crisp and crunchy to eat raw, or can be cooked in 2 minutes. Choose lentil, mung bean or similar sprouts to grow and use for the recipes in this book, not alfafa sprouts which are almost as thin as hair.

# Soy Beans and Soy Products

Soy beans and some soy products are the best vegetable foods of all for protein value. Whole soy beans are tricky to cook because they ferment easily so you may not have seen them, but almost everyone eats soy flour, usually without knowing it. It is used as a 'filler' in dozens of commercially processed foods, from pork sausages to vegetarian 'mock meat' mixes. These mixes, by the way, vary a lot in their contents, so you always need to read the label on the packet carefully to be sure you are getting foods and flavours you like. If wisely chosen, however, they certainly provide quick protein meals.

Soy sauce is probably the best known soy product in the West. It is a salty, strong-flavoured condiment used like Worcestershire sauce, although less pungent. Some brands are processed with chemicals and other additives, but top-quality Japanese soy sauce is made just from soy beans, wheat, yeast and salt processed slowly

and naturally for months. Its finer flavour makes
it worth searching for; look for the Kikkoman
label, for instance. Tamari soy sauce is another
slowly-processed soy sauce, but is made without
wheat so has a different, less rounded flavour.

Another soy product now made commercially
in the West is the soybean curd called tofu. It can
be bought as a dry 'mix' to make up yourself, as
ready-made firm tofu which looks like Mozzarella
cheese and must be kept chilled, or as softer
'silken' tofu which is like junket and is sold in a
long-life carton. Neither firm nor silken tofu have
any real flavour but both have many uses. Firm
tofu can be marinated (page 26) and the spicy
curd can then be cubed and added to vegetables,
salads or soups. Silken tofu, when whisked,
makes a good low-fat cream substitute for adding
to a fruit or vegetable purée or to mayonnaise.

# Fresh Vegetables

Potatoes are another good source of vegetable
protein, especially if teamed with eggs. When
mashed, they can also be used as a quickly made
low-fat sauce base like tofu.

Fresh vegetables together with grains and
pulses should be the basis of any vegetarian meal.
However, if you have only half an hour to make
the meal in, preparing and then cooking
vegetables such as fresh beans or peas 'from
scratch' is out of the question. Frozen, canned or
dried vegetables are therefore suggested in this
book where using them will make it practical to
produce a particular dish or will help you
materially to cut corners.

Unless frozen or other processed vegetables
are specified, always use fresh vegetables in the

recipes if you can; the timing allows for it even if, to save space, a recipe does not mention the basic washing, trimming, scraping and other preparation needed.

# Margarine, Oil and Fats

Margarine and oil are suggested for cooking in this book. They are only used sparingly because modern medical scientists suggest that most people on a Western diet should cut down their intake of fats, especially the ones we call saturated fats (strictly fats rich in saturated fatty acids). Both saturated and the main alternative polyunsaturated fats exist side by side in most fatty foods; but, generally speaking, foods of animal origin such as butter, cream, eggs and cheese contain mostly saturated fats while fish and plant oils, peanut butter and other vegetable fats contain mostly polyunsaturated fats. Thus margarine made from plant oils is likely to be high in polyunsaturates (and usually the packet label tells you so). Sunflower, soya, corn and groundnut oils, and olive oil, all contain a lot of unsaturated fatty acids. Choose which you like; only make sure you get pure, not blended, oil which may have less desirable oils mixed in. If you want to be quite certain that your margarine or cooking oil contains no animal fats at all, choose one of the types recommended for vegans in Health Food stores. You can also get suitable vegan substitutes for white fat and suet.

A point to remember is that nuts give you a nourishment 'package' containing protein and other valuable nutrients as well as a lot of fat, so they are a good way to take in the fat you need. Not all nuts, however! Coconuts and cashew nuts contain a lot of saturated fats.

Incidentally, to reduce your total fat intake painlessly, it is not a bad idea to use (or make) slimmers' low-calorie mayonnaise; normal mayonnaise and salad cream are extremely fatty foods, being made mainly of eggs (rich in saturated fats) and assorted oils. Whisk some silken tofu into commercially-made 'low-cal' mayonnaise or dressing to make it less fatty still.

Cheese, being concentrated milk, is another very fatty food but its instant flavouring value makes a small quantity well worth using sometimes. For quick use in cooking, ready-grated Cheddar and Parmesan are sold in packets and cartons respectively, and they go further than shredded or slivered solid cheese.

A low-fat type of Cheddar and one or two other hard cheeses are sold in solid portions, and so are fat-reduced soft cheeses which parallel the Petit-Suisse and Philadelphia-style cheeses. A softer, low-fat smooth curd cheese not unlike Ricotta can be bought by quantity: do not confuse it with the more expensive, full-fat type which used to be called 'cream cheese'. Unlike the rich French similar-textured cheeses, none of these soft cheeses have any special flavour; only their fat content and smooth texture distinguish them from cottage cheese.

Natural (unflavoured) low fat yoghurt is a valuable substitute for soured cream or mayonnaise; swirl it on soups, spice it and use it as a salad dressing, or sweeten it as a basis for desserts. In this book, it is measured as a liquid although the carton usually gives its weight because it is generally easier to measure it in a jug than as a solid.

# Honey and Sweeteners

Honey is used as often as sugar for sweetening in this book. Medical experts, in general, believe that we all eat too many foods loaded with sugar, and should cut out foods which consist wholly or mostly of sugar without other nutrients. Honey, like golden or corn syrup and treacle (molasses), is just sugar, but it is a bit less easy to scatter liberally than sugar, and its lovely flavour makes it seem more satisfying although you use slightly less of it. Use clear honey, slightly warmed first; you will measure the liquid warmed honey more easily, and it will spread further although you will put a bit less than usual in the spoon.

The natural fruit spread (sometimes called a pure fruit spread) which features in one or two recipes is also virtually just sugar, and even more concentrated (and costly) than honey. However, a spread does give you the fruit's flavour, and a little of it sweetens a whole dish, especially if you dilute it with water. Various brands of sugarless sweetener are also sold.

The best way to add sweetness to your meals is with whole fresh or dried fruit, but a spoonful of honey, fruit spread or unrefined brown sugar as a topping or flavouring is at least less of a health hazard than swilling back a sticky sweet drink with a slice of iced gâteau.

# Processed Foods

If you had nothing else to do, you could make superb meals just with fresh vegetables; but even then, to be properly fed, you should add whole-grain flour and rice, which are, to some extent, processed foods. Low-fat cheeses, vegetable oils, tofu and many other valuable products are only available to most of us as processed foods made by modern methods. Using frozen and canned pre-prepared vegetables, dried pre-prepared onions, herbs, minced garlic and other flavourings to speed up your cooking is really no different, provided their nutrients are intact and they have been prepared without added chemicals.

Nutritionists generally accept that plain frozen vegetables may even be better for you than tired old, so-called fresh vegetables trundled from grower to market, then to a store, and, finally, to your kitchen rack. Plain canned vegetables, although heat-treated, only need a short cooking time when you get them so offer no real extra risk of nutrient loss. Do, however, always read the list of ingredients on a can or package before you buy it, to make sure you are not getting, for instance, 'hidden' sugar or a chemical flavour-enhancer you do not want. The same applies to dried flavourings, bottled French Dressing and tomato purée.

Vegetable stock cubes are made with chemical preservatives but if you want the flavour of stock rather than water and have no spare hours to spend making it daily, you must use them. Home-made stock involves long simmering of the vegetables, and does not keep well. If you have time to make stock and freeze it in handy quantities, then this is obviously best.

Canned fruits, like canned vegetables, widen your choice of dishes, and save you precious time by being ready-prepared. Just make sure that they are canned in water, natural juice or fruit juice, not in syrup.

One last point about using canned, frozen, dried and other pre-prepared foods when you are pushed for time. If you cannot get the exact sizes of packets or cans recommended in this book, don't worry; use the size you can lay hands on most easily. Speedy shopping may well be just as important to you as quick cooking; if so, two 285 g/10 oz packets of sliced frozen beans will do just as well as one 454 g/1 lb packet. Within reason, an extra or slightly reduced quantity is not critical as a rule.

By the same token, if you have home-made vegetable stock to hand, don't make it from a cube because your recipe suggests it; use what you've got. Your meal will be all the tastier.

# BASIC BACKSTOPS

It seems odd to start a book on quick meals with recipes which take some time to cook, but unless you are going to eat entirely out of packets and cans, supplemented by bread, 'instant' pasta and fried chips, you need to be able to prepare ahead of time at least a small choice of cooked grains and pulses on which to base freshly-cooked vegetables and sauces. If you drain them well and freeze them in polythene bags, they thaw in a few minutes when reheated. Most beans (although not soy beans) even keep well in a refrigerator for two or three days in a sealed container without losing their food value. You will find any of the basic 'backstops' below worth while.

## Cooking Pulses

Pulses such as split red lentils need not soak before being boiled. Others such as black-eyed beans need only soak in boiling water for an hour, and then boil gently for about 45 minutes. A few pulses, notably soya beans, whole peas and chickpeas need several hours' soaking and simmering; but soya beans in particular are such good value that they are well worth the trouble.

Cook all pulses in their soaking water. Unlike other plant foods, cook them ahead of time because each batch varies. Test by tasting for the last half-hour of the cooking time; drain and salt them as soon as they are tender. (Do not salt them before cooking; it toughens the skins.)

If you have the chance, always pressure-cook pulses (except red lentils and split peas); they look and taste better as well as cooking faster.

17

## SOAKING AND BOILING TIMES FOR PULSES

| Type of Pulse | Soaking Time | Average Boiling time |
|---|---|---|
| Adzuki beans | 6 hrs or overnight | 1½-2 hrs |
| Black-eyed beans | 1-1½ hrs | 45 minutes |
| Butter beans | Overnight | 2 hrs |
| Haricot beans | Overnight | 1½-2 hrs |
| Mung beans | 2-4 hrs | 20-30 minutes |
| Red kidney beans | Overnight | 2-2½ hrs |
| Soya beans | Overnight, refrigerated | 3½-4 hrs |
| Chickpeas | Overnight | 3 hrs |
| Split peas | — | 35 minutes |
| Whole dried peas | 4 hrs | 1½-2 hrs |
| Brown lentils | 4 hrs | 1 hr |
| Split red lentils | — | 20-30 minutes |
| Whole red lentils | 1 hr | 30-40 minutes |

Any beans freeze well. Cool, then package them in bags or boxes, in serving portions. Reheat by tipping into boiling water and cooking, when back on the boil, for a few minutes; otherwise, simmer with melted fat in a saucepan, or reheat in a covered shallow dish with a few spoonfuls of stock in a low oven.

# Cooking Soya Beans

Soya beans are such a valuable food, they are worth the extra care they need. Refrigerate them while soaking because they ferment easily; you may need to top up the soaking water since they swell considerably. For the same reason, cook them in a really large pan, and top up the cooking water from time to time, stirring round when you do so. The beans should be swollen, glossy and tender when ready. Drain off any free liquid, season the beans and mix them with melted fat and a few chopped herbs.

# Cooking Wholemeal and Spinach Pasta

Wholemeal pasta, like brown rice, contains valuable nutrients and fibre missing from white pasta. All types and shapes of pasta are cooked in plain boiling, slightly salted water; the main seasoning is added with the sauce or other food served with or over the pasta. Some pasta, such as cannelloni and lasagne are only parboiled, because they are then used for oven-baked dishes.

Allow about 85 g/$3\frac{1}{2}$ oz pasta for each main-course helping of boiled pasta served with a sauce. Bring a large pan of water to a fast boil; the pasta strands must be able to separate. Add a mere sprinkling of salt. Put one end of long pasta rods into the water, and push them down gently against the pan bottom as they soften; add only a small number at a time so that the water does not go off the boil. Drop 'nests' or coils of thin pasta or flat noodles into the water and stir them round with a fork to separate them. Scatter small flat shapes into the water. Boil the pasta, uncovered until it has lost any floury taste; it must be tender but not mushy. Here are the approximate times to cook it for.

## COOKING TIMES FOR PASTA

| Type of Pasta | Cooking time |
| --- | --- |
| Thin strands, e.g. vermicelli | 5 minutes |
| Flat or thinnish strands, e.g. spaghetti, tagliatelli | 7-10 minutes |
| Tubular thinnish strands, e.g. macaroni | 12-20 minutes |
| Fancy shapes and short lengths, e.g. shells, elbow macaroni | 8-10 minutes |
| Large tubes, e.g. cannelloni, rigatoni | 16-20 minutes |
| Tiny shapes for soup, e.g. stars, alphabet | 4-8 minutes |

Test whether the pasta is ready about 2 minutes before it should be by nibbling a strand. If it is not, test after another 2 minutes. When it is done, drain it in a large colander. If you will use it at once, return it to the dry pan with a knob of fat, and leave it at the side of the stove until you want to use it. If it must wait longer than 5 minutes, put it in a round-bottomed sieve lined with a damp cloth, and place it over hot water; cover it with greased paper.

To freeze it, undercook it slightly, cool, then combine it if you wish with a sauce or a little melted fat and pack it in a rigid container. Seal and fast-freeze. To defrost and reheat the pasta, tip it into boiling water for about 1 minute, or (if sauced) placed the covered container in a fairly hot oven until heated through. The time will depend on the quantity and thickness of the pasta.

Wholemeal and green (spinach) pasta cook in the same time. Some pasta shapes of both kinds are pre-cooked, dried and sold as 'instant' or

'4-minute' pasta. Follow the cooking instructions on the package.

Any long pasta can be served just with melted fat and grated cheese or with a sauce. Several recipes in later sections contain suitable sauces. See the Index.

## Cooking Brown Rice

Brown rice contains most nutrients which human bodies need. You can get long and short grain rice and a sweetish type which is slightly more glutinous when cooked. Any cooked brown rice keeps well for 4-5 days in a refrigerator or even in a cold larder, so it is worth cooking a week's supply at a time.

# Brown Rice

Cooking time: 25 minutes (V)

| **INGREDIENTS** | Metric | Imperial | American |
|---|---|---|---|
| Brown rice (any type) | 225 g | 8 oz | 1 cup (rounded) |
| Water as needed | | | |
| Oil (see page 13) | 2 tsp | 2 tsp | 2 tsp |

Rinse the rice in a strainer under cold running water. Put it in a pan, and add enough water to cover the rice with a good 8 cm/3 in clear water. Add the oil. Bring to the boil, cover the pan and reduce the heat to simmering. Simmer for 25-35 minutes until the rice is tender but still chewy. Drain off any remaining water. If not needed at once, cool in the strainer, and pack in a sealed polythene bag for freezing or refrigerating. Reheat like beans.

Rice is the grain most often used whole. Other grains such as oats, rye, barley, millet and maize are usually processed as chips, flakes, large or small granules, meal or flour. For instance rolled to flaked oats or oatmeal are used for making porridge. Most of these grains take too long to cook properly as 'basics' for half-hour menu-making, but you will find recipes for bulghar (partly-milled wheat parboiled, then dried) and for polenta (maize meal) on pages 49 and 59, plus ideas for using some other grains below.

# Cooking Stewed Fruit

Stewed fruit is an easy 'make-ahead' to have hot or cold for breakfast or as a dessert next day, or to freeze. Most ripe fruits do not really need sweetening. But if you want sweetened fruit, add dried fruit such as dates or sultanas, or poach the fruit in water mixed with natural apple or other fruit juice. As a luxury, you could use sweet white wine or ginger wine instead of fruit juice, or flavour the water with a little sweet liqueur. NONE OF THESE ARE SUGAR-FREE and none are cheap, but because of their flavour, you tend to use less of them than sugar. Natural maple syrup or clear honey are other alternatives.

Spices also add interest to stewed fruit, for instance if you have a glut of autumn apples and want to vary them. A pinch of ground cinnamon, allspice or grated nutmeg, or a strip of lemon rind, add a piquant flavour.

Soft fruits such as raspberries do not need cooking in the sweetened liquid at all; just pour the hot liquid over them, and let them soak. Most other fruits need processing once they are cut up, to soften them or prevent them discolouring. Bring the water or sweetened liquid to the boil, then take it off the heat. Prepare the fruit, e.g. remove stones, pips and cores, and put the fruit in the liquid at once. Replace over very gentle heat, cover the pan and simmer very gently until the fruit is tender. The time will vary with the quality and type of fruit, but always cook it for as short a time as possible.

Use only just enough liquid to cover the fruit. When the fruit is ready, lift it out into a heatproof bowl with a slotted spoon, then strain some or all of the liquid over it. Serve hot or cold, alone or with muesli.

# BREAKFAST SPECIALS

Nutritionists generally recommend taking in a proportion of all the various nutrients you need early in the day. The Swiss dish, Muesli, is a marvellously tasty way to get them, and to get yourself going. You can vary it in dozen of ways. Some other breakfast ideas for the young, the hungry or just the very late Sunday risers are listed in the Index.

## Making Muesli

Properly made modern muesli is one of the best breakfasts you can have. It is an almost complete food, consisting of crushed dry or soaked grain, fresh raw fruit and/or dried fruit and nuts, eaten with milk, a milk substitute or whole milk yoghurt, and sweetened if you wish. Several commercial dry muesli mixes are sold to which you can add your own fresh ingredients; but home-made muesli is more interesting because it can be varied by using so many different grains and flavourings. Here are some of the choices:

**Grains:** Oatflakes, flaked wheat, barley, millet or soya flakes.
**Fruit:** Chopped dried apples, pears, apricots, plums; well-drained fresh orange segments or chopped fresh pineapple; chopped fresh apricots or plums dipped in lemon juice; pipped grapes; whole fresh soft fruits; dates, raisins, sultanas or dried chopped figs.
**Liquid:** Milk, or soya milk; single or whipping cream; natural low-fat or whole milk yoghurt; cultured buttermilk.

# Store-Cupboard Muesli

Preparation time (ahead): 10 minutes; (at serving point): 5 minutes (V)

| INGREDIENTS | Metric | Imperial | American |
| --- | --- | --- | --- |
| Seeded raisins or dried apricots | 25 g | 1 oz | 1 oz |
| Sultanas | 25 g | 1 oz | 1 oz |
| Rolled oats or wheat flakes | 125 g | 4 oz | 4 oz |
| Chopped mixed nuts, almonds or Brazil nuts | 3 tbsp | 3 tbsp | 3 tbsp |
| Unrefined golden granulated sugar (optional) | 25 g | 1 oz | 1oz |
| **Added at serving point** | | | |
| Large sharp dessert apple | 1 | 1 | 1 |
| Lemon juice | | | |
| Natural low-fat or whole milk yoghurt or soya milk | 2 tbsp | 2 tbsp | 2 tbsp |
| Honey or diluted natural apricot spread (optional) | | | |

Up to a week before use, chop the raisins or apricots, and mix with the sultanas, rolled oats and nuts. Mix in the sugar if you wish, unless you will use honey. Store in a sealed container.

Just before serving, core and dice the apple and toss it in lemon juice. Whisk the yoghurt with the honey if using it. Turn the stored ingredients into a bowl, and mix in the other ingredients. Serve in small porringers.

# Making Savoury Tofu

A boiled egg is the quickest and easiest hot breakfast to make if you do not want porridge or stewed fruit. But if you want to keep down your intake of eggs or to avoid them altogether, grilled marinated tofu (below) makes an unusual but satisfying pre-prepared alternative which can be used in several ways at other meals too. It is good-tempered as well since it will keep for at least a week in the refrigerator in its soaking 'mix'.

## Marinated Tofu

Preparation time: 5 minutes   Cooking time (for
grilled tofu): 3 minutes                          (V)

| INGREDIENTS | Metric | Imperial | American |
|---|---|---|---|
| *Block of firm tofu (283.5 g/10 oz)* | *1* | *1* | *1* |
| **For the Marinade** | | | |
| *Soy sauce* | *2 tbsp* | *2 tbsp* | *2 tbsp* |
| *Sherry* | *3 tbsp* | *3 tbsp* | *3 tbsp* |
| *Brown sugar (unrefined if possible)* | *1 tbsp* | *1 tbsp* | *1 tbsp* |
| *Ground ginger* | *1 tsp* | *1 tsp* | *1 tsp* |
| *Oil (see page 13)* | *1 tbsp* | *1 tbsp* | *1 tbsp* |
| *Garlic clove, squeezed* | *½* | *½* | *½* |
| *OR Dried minced garlic* | *¼ tsp* | *¼ tsp* | *¼ tsp* |
| *Dry mustard powder* | *¼ tsp* | *¼ tsp* | *¼ tsp* |

Drain the tofu on a tilted plate while you make the marinade by mixing all the ingredients together. Put the tofu in a container which just holds it, and pour the marinade over it. Leave it in the refrigerator for at least 24 hours, longer if possible, turning it over daily to soak both sides.

## TO GRILL TOFU
Place a block of drained, marinated tofu on a piece of foil in the grill pan. Heat the grill while you brush the surface of the tofu with oil. Put it under the grill for 1–2 minutes until it bubbles. Remove the pan from the heat at once, or the tofu will toughen. If you wish, turn the tofu over and grill the other side like the first.

## TO SERVE TOFU
Cut plain marinated or grilled tofu into slices, or slit a thick block through the centre horizontally, and cut both parts into fingers or small cubes.

## NOTES
For breakfast or to use the tofu as a salad ingredient, marinate it in a single block as above; when it is cut up, the white surfaces will not be flavoured. To use cubed tofu for cocktail snack or in a dish of mixed vegetables, slit the tofu through the centre before marinating it, and lay the thin sheets side by side in the marinade. Both sides of each small cube will then be flavoured.

Cubes of grilled, marinated tofu make a good substitute for cheese in a salad.

For other dishes suitable for breakfast, see Polenta (page 59), Spiced Bulghar (page 49) and Stir-Fried Potato Slices with Sage (page 56).

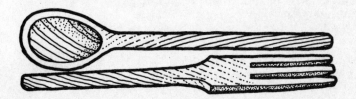

27

# Cooking Porridge

The quickest way to have hot porridge for breakfast is to start it cooking the night before. It can cook gently all night on some solid fuel stoves, but for most of us, the easiest and cheapest way to make it is in a wide-necked insulated food flask - always a good investment anyway.

## Thermos Porridge

Cooking time: 5 minutes   Serves 2                  Ⓥ

| INGREDIENTS | Metric | Imperial | American |
|---|---|---|---|
| *Coarse oatmeal* | *8 tbsp* | *8 tbsp* | *8 tbsp* |
| *Water* | *425 ml* | *¾ pt* | *2 cups* |
| *Seedless raisins* | *1 tbsp* | *1 tbsp* | *1 tbsp* |
| *Salt* | *¼ tsp* | *¼ tsp* | *¼ tsp* |

Put all the ingredients in a saucepan, and bring slowly to the boil. Cook gently, uncovered, for 5 minutes, stirring often. While cooking, rinse out a wide-mouthed insulated food flask with boiling water. Tip in the porridge, stopper the flask securely and leave for 8-10 hours. Turn it out, spoon it into bowls, mash to break it up if needed, and serve with milk or cream (or a vegan alternative such as soya milk). Sweeten if you wish.

**NOTE**
You could add sliced bananas for extra nourishment.

# MAIN COURSE DISHES WITHOUT DAIRY FOODS

## Pacific Chop Suey

Cooking time: 12 minutes ⓥ

| INGREDIENTS | Metric | Imperial | American |
|---|---|---|---|
| Onion | 175 g | 6 oz | 6 oz |
| Celery stalks | 175 g | 6 oz | 6 oz |
| White cabbage (segment) | 75 g | 3 oz | 3 oz |
| Can of pineapple in natural juice (22 g/8 oz) | 1 | 1 | 1 |
| Oil for frying (see page 13) | 3 tbsp | 3 tbsp | 3 tbsp |
| Vegetable stock | 3 tbsp | 3 tbsp | 3 tbsp |
| Bean sprouts | 125 g | 4 oz | 4 oz |
| Flaked almonds or Brazil nuts | 25 g | 1 oz | ¼ cup |
| Soy sauce | 2 tbsp | 2 tbsp | 2 tbsp |
| Reheated brown rice (see page 22) | 500 g | 18 oz | 3 cups |

Chop the onion and celery finely, and shred the cabbage. Drain and chop the pineapple coarsely (use the juice for a dessert). Heat a (dry) deep frying pan (skillet) with a lid or spatter-proof cover. Add the oil, onion, celery and cabbage when it is hot. Stir over moderate heat for 3 minutes. Add the vegetable stock, cover and steam-cook for 5 minutes. Stir in the chopped pineapple, bean sprouts, flaked nuts and soy sauce. Steam for another 4 minutes; uncover and stir once while steaming. When hot, serve quickly over reheated brown rice.

# Curried Potato Garland

Cooking time: 10 minutes         Ⓥ

| **INGREDIENTS** | Metric | Imperial | American |
|---|---|---|---|
| Instant potato powder or granules (1 large pkt) | 150 g | 5 oz | 5 oz |
| Curry powder | ¼ tsp | ¼ tsp | ¼ tsp |
| A few grains of cayenne pepper | | | |
| Pkt of frozen mixed vegetables (454 g/1 lb) | 1 | 1 | 1 |
| Salt and ground black pepper (optional) | | | |
| Tomato purée | 1 tsp | 1 tsp | 1 tsp |
| Water | 275 ml | ½ pt | 1¼ cups |
| Milk or soya milk | 175 ml | 6 fl oz | ¾ cup |
| Margarine (see page 13) | 3 tbsp | 3 tbsp | 3 tbsp |

Mix in a bowl the dried potato, curry powder and cayenne pepper.

Cook the frozen mixed vegetables according to the packet directions; when ready, drain and season if you wish. Keep warm. While cooking, blend the tomato purée into the water in a saucepan. Add the milk and 2 tbsp of the fat, and heat to boiling point. Reconstitute the potato with the liquid, and leave to stand while you pile the vegetables in the middle of a warmed serving platter. Spoon the curried potato into a ring around them. Dot the vegetables with the remaining fat, and serve at once.

# Spectrum Stir-Fry

Cooking time: 15 minutes     Ⓥ

| INGREDIENTS | Metric | Imperial | American |
|---|---|---|---|
| Medium-sized leek, green and white parts | 1 | 1 | 1 |
| Can of sweetcorn with peppers (198 g/7 oz) | 1 | 1 | 1 |
| Cooked or canned red kidney beans (213 g/ 7½ oz can) | 125 g | 4 oz | 4 oz |
| Medium-sized carrot | 1 | 1 | 1 |
| Spring onions (scallions), green and white parts | 4 | 4 | 4 |
| Celery stalks | 2 | 2 | 2 |
| Sherry | 1 tbsp | 1 tbsp | 1 tbsp |
| Soy sauce | 1 tbsp | 1 tbsp | 1 tbsp |
| Tomato juice | 1 tbsp | 1 tbsp | 1 tbsp |
| Water | 1 tbsp | 1 tbsp | 1 tbsp |
| Oil (see page 13) | 3 tbsp | 3 tbsp | 3 tbsp |

Heat enough water to cook the leek when sliced. Slice, add it to the pan on the boil, and cook it for 5 minutes. Meanwhile, drain the corn and beans if needed. Put in a bowl; drain and add the cooked leek. Chop the carrot, spring onions and celery coarsely, in a food processor if possible. Mix all the liquids in a jug.

Heat the oil in a deep frying pan. Add the carrot, onions and celery, and stir over medium heat for 2 minutes. Add the leek, sweetcorn and beans, and continue stirring for 3 minutes. Add the liquids, cover the pan and simmer for 2 minutes or until it is all absorbed.

# Record-Quick 'Ratatouille'

Cooking time: 10 minutes      ⓥ

| **INGREDIENTS** | Metric | Imperial | American |
|---|---|---|---|
| *Large onions* | 2 | 2 | 2 |
| *Medium-sized sweet red pepper* | 1 | 1 | 1 |
| *Medium-sized yellow pepper or green pepper* | 1 | 1 | 1 |
| *Medium-sized green pepper* | 1 | 1 | 1 |
| *Courgettes (zucchini)* | 450 g | 1 lb | 1 lb |
| *'Instant' whole wheat noodles (see page 20)* | 225 g | 8 oz | ½ lb |
| *Olive oil* | 2 tbsp | 2 tbsp | 2 tbsp |
| *Can of chopped tomatoes in juice* | 400 g | 14 oz | 14 oz |
| *Salt and ground black pepper* | | | |

While preparing the vegetables, bring a large pan of water to the boil. Chop the onions. De-seed the peppers. Slice or chop the peppers and courgettes, whichever is quickest.

Tip the noodles and 1 tsp of the oil into the water, and stir round. Cook for 4 minutes, then remove from the heat.

While cooking the pasta, heat the rest of the oil in a large, deep frying pan with a lid or spatter-proof cover. Add the onions, and stir over medium heat for 2 minutes. Add the other fresh vegetables and stir, turning them over, for another 3 minutes. Add the tomatoes and their juice, cover the pan and cook gently for 5 minutes or until the vegetables are crisp-tender.

Drain the pasta. Season both pasta and vegetables. Turn the vegetables onto a warmed platter, and spoon the pasta around them.

**NOTES**
If you are not going to serve beans, peas or lentils elsewhere in the meal, you could cook 175 g/6 oz pasta together with 113 g/4 oz frozen broad beans straight from the packet. Cook for 5 minutes.

Add 1 tsp dried basil or thyme with the tomatoes if you have time.

# Stuffed Cabbage Leaves

Cooking time: 12 minutes                                    Ⓥ

| **INGREDIENTS** | Metric | Imperial | American |
|---|---|---|---|
| *Large cabbage leaves* | *4* | *4* | *4* |
| *Vegetable stock* | *175-225 ml* | *6-8 fl oz* | *¾-1 cup* |
| *Hera vegetarian burger or meatball 'mix' (dry weight of 1 sachet)* | *100 g* | *3½ oz* | *3½ oz* |
| *Small onion* | *1* | *1* | *1* |
| *Small tomato* | *1* | *1* | *1* |
| *Oil (see page 13)* | *3 tbsp* | *3 tbsp* | *3 tbsp* |

Lay the cabbage leaves flat in a frying pan, and pour in about 2 cm/¾ in depth of stock. Cover the pan with a spatterproof cover or plate, and simmer the leaves for 2-3 minutes until soft. Remove the leaves and lay them flat, side by side, leaving the stock in the pan.

Reconstitute the sachet of 'mix' as the packet instructions direct and leave to stand. While it stands, chop the onion and tomato. Heat 2 tbsp of the oil in a second, fairly large frying pan, and sauté the chopped vegetables for 2 minutes. Add the 'mix' and the remaining oil and stir for another 2 minutes.

Cool for 1 minute, then divide the 'mix' between the cabbage leaves, laying it in a line down the centre rib of each leaf; roll the leaf round it like a tube. Return the rolls to the pan containing the stock, placing them cut side down. Pour in more stock if needed to prevent drying out while reheating. Cover, and simmer for about 3 minutes to heat the rolls through well. Place them on a warmed serving dish, and spoon a little hot stock over them. Serve with mashed potato (instant if you are short of time) or Rose Red Potatoes (see page 57).

**NOTE**
For man-sized appetites, double all the main ingredient quantities and use extra stock and oil as required. A packet of 'mix' contains 2 sachets.


# Corncrust Tart

Cooking time: 25 minutes                          Ⓧ Ⓥ

| **INGREDIENTS** | Metric | Imperial | American |
| --- | --- | --- | --- |
| **For the case (made ahead)** | | | |
| *Fine maize meal (cornmeal)* | *225 g* | *8 oz* | *1²⁄₃ cups* |
| *Salt (optional)* | *¼ tsp* | *¼ tsp* | *¼ tsp* |
| *Oil (see page 13)* | | | |
| *Cold vegetable stock (see method)* | | | |

**For the filling**

| | | | |
|---|---|---|---|
| Cooked or canned flageolet (green lima) beans, drained | 175 g | 6 oz | 1 cup |
| Medium-sized onion | 1 | 1 | 1 |
| Medium-sized carrot | 1 | 1 | 1 |
| Celery stalks | 50 g | 2 oz | 2 oz |
| Green pepper, de-seeded | ½ | ½ | ½ |
| Garlic clove | ½ | ½ | ½ |
| Oil (see page 13) | 2 tbsp | 2 tbsp | 2 tbsp |
| Ground cumin | 1 tsp | 1 tsp | 1 tsp |
| Tabasco | 3 drops | 3 drops | 3 drops |

Ahead of time, mix together the maize meal, salt (if used), oil and enough liquid to make a firm paste. This will depend on the type of maize meal and the mixing method you use, but you will probably need at least 100 ml/4 fl oz. Press the paste all over the base and sides of a well-oiled 23 cm/9 in pie plate.

To cook, heat the oven to 180°C/350°F/Gas Mark 4. Place the tart case in the oven to 'set'. Drain the beans if needed. Chop finely together, in a food processor if possible, the onion, carrot, celery, pepper and garlic. Sauté the chopped vegetables in 2 tbsp oil for 4 minutes. Stir in the beans, cumin and Tabasco. Fill the mixture into the hot maize meal case, and return to the oven for 10–15 minutes until the case is firm and the filling well heated.

**NOTES**
If you have time, spread a 227 g/8 oz can of chopped plum tomatoes over the filling before baking.

This dish takes too long to make for a three-course menu in 30 minutes.

# Creamed Cauliflower Supper

Cooking time: 10 minutes          (V)

| **INGREDIENTS** | Metric | Imperial | American |
|---|---|---|---|
| Vegetable stock cube | 1 | 1 | 1 |
| Pinch of dried minced garlic | | | |
| Medium-sized thin-skinned potatoes | 350 g | 12 oz | 3/4 lb |
| Cauliflower florets | 450 g | 1 lb | 1 lb |
| Carton of silken tofu (297 g) | 1 | 1 | 1 |
| White wine vinegar | 1 1/2 tsp | 1 1/2 tsp | 1 1/2 tsp |
| Good pinch of dry mustard | | | |
| A few drops of Tabasco | | | |
| Salt | 1/8 tsp | 1/8 tsp | 1/8 tsp |
| Dill seeds | | | |

Put two medium-sized pans of water to heat. Add the vegetable stock cube to one, and sprinkle the dried minced garlic into the other. Cut the potatoes into 5 mm/1/4 in slices and add to the pan with the stock cube as soon as the water boils. Bring back to the boil, and cook for 6 minutes or until the slices are just tender; drain and spread in an even layer in a shallow 20 cm/8 in pie plate or baking dish. Keep warm.

Tip the cauliflower florets into the pan with the garlic when on the boil, bring back to boiling, and cook for 8-10 minutes until tender. While cooking, drain the tofu, and whisk it in a bowl with the vinegar, mustard, Tabasco and salt until creamy. Drain the cauliflower when ready, and mash it into the tofu mixture. Taste and adjust the seasoning. Spread the creamed cauliflower over the potato, and sprinkle with dill seeds.

# Savoy Casserole

Cooking time: 18 minutes  Ⓧ Ⓥ

| INGREDIENTS | Metric | Imperial | American |
|---|---|---|---|
| Onions | 100 g | 4 oz | 4 oz |
| Medium-sized carrots | 2 | 2 | 2 |
| Savoy cabbage | 700 g | 1½ lb | 1½ lb |
| Medium-sized leek | 1 | 1 | 1 |
| Oil (see page 13) | 3 tbsp | 3 tbsp | 3 tbsp |
| Water | 150 ml | ¼ pt | ½ cup + 2 tbsp |
| Raisins | 50 g | 2 oz | ⅓ cup |
| Caraway seeds | ½ tsp | ½ tsp | ½ tsp |
| Wholemeal (whole wheat) breadcrumbs | 3 tbsp | 3 tbsp | 3 tbsp |
| Cider vinegar | 3 tbsp | 3 tbsp | 3 tbsp |
| Honey | 2 tsp | 2 tsp | 2 tsp |
| Salt and ground black pepper | | | |

Chop the onions and carrots coarsely. Core and
slice the cabbage, and slice the leek. In a large
pan, sauté the onions and carrots in 2 tbsp of the
oil until the onion softens. Mix in the remaining
oil, and the cabbage and leek, stirring well. Add 2
tbsp of the water, and cover the pan; reduce the
heat, and simmer for 4 minutes. Stir in the
raisins, seeds and breadcrumbs, and the
remaining water with the vinegar and honey.
Cover again, and simmer for another 10-12
minutes, stirring once or twice. The dish is ready
when the vegetables are soft and the liquids
absorbed. Season to taste before serving.

Stir-Fried Potato Slices with Sage (page 56)
go well with the cabbage.

# Memory Stew

Cooking time: 17 minutes (V)

| INGREDIENTS | Metric | Imperial | American |
|---|---|---|---|
| Young French (snap) beans, topped and tailed ahead, or frozen sliced green beans | 275 g approx | 10 oz approx | 10 oz approx |
| Vegetable stock | 275 ml | ½ pt | 1¼ cups |
| Can of sweetcorn (198 g/7 oz) | 1 | 1 | 1 |
| Spring onions (scallions), green and white parts | 4 | 4 | 4 |
| Medium-sized tomatoes | 3 | 3 | 3 |
| Medium-sized eating apple | 1 | 1 | 1 |
| Dried rosemary | 1 tsp | 1 tsp | 1 tsp |
| Finely chopped walnut pieces | 50 g | 2 oz | ⅓ cup |
| Salt and ground black pepper (optional) | | | |

Cook the beans in the stock, in a covered pan, for 7 minutes. While cooking, open the can of corn, and cut the spring onions into 1 cm/½ in lengths. Quarter the tomatoes. Quarter, core and peel the apple, then chop it roughly.

Add the corn and its juice, and all the other ingredients to the pan of beans. Mix well, cover again, and cook until the vegetables are tender, stirring once or twice.

# Steamed Vegetable Fruits

Cooking time: 16 minutes      Ⓥ

| **INGREDIENTS** | Metric | Imperial | American |
|---|---|---|---|
| *Shallots* | *3* | *3* | *3* |
| *Medium-sized courgettes (zucchini)* | *2* | *2* | *2* |
| *Medium-sized aubergine (eggplant)* | *1* | *1* | *1* |
| *Oil (see page 13)* | | | |
| *Medium-sized tomatoes* | *3* | *3* | *3* |
| *Large garlic clove* | *1* | *1* | *1* |
| *Water* | *4 tbsp* | *4 tbsp* | *4 tbsp* |
| *A few drops of soy sauce* | | | |
| *Salt (optional)* | | | |
| *Large square slices wholemeal (whole wheat) bread* | *2* | *2* | *2* |

Peel and slice the shallots. Slice the unpeeled
courgettes and aubergine into rounds. Heat the oil
in a deep frying pan (skillet) with a lid, or
spatterproof cover. Add the sliced vegetables, and
sauté them for 5 minutes, turning them
constantly. Slice the tomatoes, squeeze the garlic
over them, and add them to the pan. Pour in the
water, flavoured with soy sauce. Cover tightly,
lower the heat and simmer gently for 10 minutes
or until the vegetables are soft; season after
cooking if you wish.

While cooking, toast the bread on both sides,
and cut into 8 triangles. Arrange the vegetables in
a shallow dish with the bread triangles around
them. Serve with a Mixed Pulse Salad (page 70).

# Italian Bean Sprouts

Cooking time: 17 minutes ⊗ Ⓥ

| INGREDIENTS | Metric | Imperial | American |
|---|---|---|---|
| Can of plum tomatoes in juice (396 g/ 14 oz) | 1 | 1 | 1 |
| Medium-sized onion | 1 | 1 | 1 |
| Celery (3 average stalks) | 175 g | 6 oz | 6 oz |
| Good pinch of dried minced garlic | | | |
| Button mushrooms | 75 g | 3 oz | 3 oz |
| Dried basil or marjoram | ½ tsp | ½ tsp | ½ tsp |
| Oil (see page 13) | 1 tbsp | 1 tbsp | 1 tbsp |
| Bean sprouts | 175 g | 6 oz | 6 oz |
| White wine (optional but good) | 2 tbsp | 2 tbsp | 2 tbsp |
| Salt (optional) | | | |

Drain the can of tomatoes, reserving the juice. Chop the onion, celery and garlic, in a food processor if possible. Slice the mushrooms and mix with your chosen herb. Heat the oil in a large frying pan with a spatter-proof cover or lid, and stir-fry the onion, celery and garlic for 4 minutes. Add the tomatoes and 3 tbsp of the juice, and the mushrooms. Cover, reduce the heat, and simmer for 12-13 minutes; stir in the bean sprouts, with the wine if you use it, after 10 minutes, then continue simmering, covered, for the remaining 3-4 minutes or until the bean sprouts are soft. Season after cooking if you wish.

# MAIN COURSE DISHES WITH EGGS, CHEESE, DAIRY MILK AND YOGHURT

## Sauced Green Beans and Onions

Cooking time: 15 minutes

| INGREDIENTS | Metric | Imperial | American |
|---|---|---|---|
| *Pkt of frozen sliced green beans (454 g/1 lb)* | *1* | *1* | *1* |
| *Salt and ground black pepper* | | | |
| *Large onion* | *1* | *1* | *1* |
| *Oil (see page 13)* | *3 tbsp* | *3 tbsp* | *3 tbsp* |
| *Margarine (see page 13)* | *2 tbsp* | *2 tbsp* | *2 tbsp* |
| *Wholemeal (whole wheat) flour* | *2 tbsp* | *2 tbsp* | *2 tbsp* |
| *Clear honey* | *1 tsp* | *1 tsp* | *1 tsp* |
| *Milk* | *125 ml* | *4 fl oz* | *½ cup* |
| *Natural yoghurt* | *275 ml* | *½ pt* | *1¼ cups* |

Cook the beans according to the packet direction. When ready, drain and season well. Spread them evenly in a shallow heatproof dish suitable for serving; they should fill about half the depth of the dish. Cover the dish, and keep it warm.

While cooking the beans, slice the onion thinly. Put the slices in a saucepan with 2 tbsp of the oil. Stir-fry over medium heat for 3-4 minutes until the slices soften and start to colour. Spread them on the beans, reserving any oil in the pan.

Cover again, and keep warm while you make a Yoghurt Sauce.

For the sauce, add the remaining 1 tbsp oil and all the fat to the saucepan. Melt over low heat, then add in turn, slowly, the flour, honey and milk, stirring each in thoroughly. Continue stirring until the sauce thickens; then stir in the yoghurt, and take the pan off the heat. Season lightly and spoon the sauce over the vegetables. Serve at once.

**NOTE**

If you have time, you could fry an unpeeled, thinly sliced aubergine (eggplant) with the onions. Use 2 extra tbsp oil. The slices will take a few minutes longer than the onion to soften.

Alternatively, you could sprinkle the dish with grated cheese.

# Turkish Omelette

Cooking time: 12 minutes

| INGREDIENTS | Metric | Imperial | American |
|---|---|---|---|
| *Medium-sized green pepper* | *1* | *1* | *1* |
| *Medium-sized onion* | *1* | *1* | *1* |
| *Olive oil* | *4 tbsp* | *4 tbsp* | *4 tbsp* |
| *Cucumber* | *150 g* | *5 oz* | *5 oz* |
| *Medium-sized tomatoes* | *2* | *2* | *2* |
| *Dried minced garlic* | *½ tsp* | *½ tsp* | *½ tsp* |
| *Eggs* | *4* | *4* | *4* |
| *Salt* | *¼ tsp* | *¼ tsp* | *¼ tsp* |
| *Pinch each of ground cumin and cayenne pepper* | | | |
| *Soft wholemeal (whole wheat) breadcrumbs* | *4 tbsp* | *4 tbsp* | *4 tbsp* |
| *Water* | *2 tbsp* | *2 tbsp* | *2 tbsp* |

De-seed the pepper, and chop it with the onion (in a food processor if possible). Put them in a 25 cm/10 in frying pan with the oil. Chop the cucumber and tomatoes coarsely, and mix in the garlic; keep aside.

Fry the pepper and onion over medium heat for 2 minutes, stirring once or twice. Mix in the cucumber, tomato and garlic, and stir-fry for 3 minutes. Beat the eggs in a bowl with the salt, spices, breadcrumbs and 2 tbsp water. Stir the egg mixture into the vegetables. Reduce the heat to low, cover the pan with a spatter-proof lid or plate, and simmer for 5-6 minutes until the eggs are just set. Serve in wedges from the pan.

# Dairy-Dressed Vegetables

Cooking time: 12 minutes

| INGREDIENTS | Metric | Imperial | American |
|---|---|---|---|
| Medium-sized tomatoes | 2 | 2 | 2 |
| Celery stalks | 3 | 3 | 3 |
| Small carrots | 4 | 4 | 4 |
| Cans of new potatoes in salt water (300 g each) | 3 | 3 | 3 |
| Margarine (see page 13) | 1 tbsp | 1 tbsp | 1 tbsp |
| Oil (see page 13) | 2 tbsp | 2 tbsp | 2 tbsp |
| Natural yoghurt | 150 ml | 1/4 pt | 1/2 cup + 2 tbsp |
| Mayonnaise (see page 14) | 1 tbsp | 1 tbsp | 1 tbsp |
| Salt and ground black pepper | | | |
| Grated Cheddar cheese | 75 g | 3 oz | 3/4 cup |

Slice the tomatoes and keep aside. Chop the celery and carrots finely, in a food processor if possible. Drain the canned potatoes.

Put the fat and oil in a deep frying pan, and toss the potatoes in it for 2 minutes over medium heat. Add the chopped vegetables, and stir-fry for 3 minutes. Reduce the heat to as low as possible. Mix together the yoghurt, mayonnaise and a little seasoning, and stir them into the vegetables. Leave to stand over the very low heat, well below the boil, for 3 minutes. Heat the grill.

Turn the yoghurt-coated vegetables into a flameproof serving dish, and cover with the cheese. Place under the grill for 3-4 minutes to melt the cheese. Serve at once, garnished with the tomato slices.

# Quick Stuffed Peppers

Cooking time: 17 minutes

| **INGREDIENTS** | Metric | Imperial | American |
| --- | --- | --- | --- |
| *Large sweet red peppers* | 2 | 2 | 2 |
| *Pkt of frozen mixed vegetables (peas, carrot and sweetcorn) (227 g/8 oz)* | 1 | 1 | 1 |
| *Spring onion (scallion), green and white parts* | 1 | 1 | 1 |
| *Wholemeal (whole wheat) breadcrumbs* | 25 g | 1 oz | 1 oz |
| *Grated Cheddar cheese* | 50 g | 2 oz | ½ cup |
| *Soy sauce* | 1 tbsp | 1 tbsp | 1 tbsp |
| *Small egg* | 1 | 1 | 1 |

Set the oven to heat to 190°C/375°F/Gas Mark 5. Put a large pan of water on to boil. Cut the peppers in half lengthways, remove the cores and seeds, and cook in the boiling water for 8 minutes. Drain.

While they boil, cook the frozen vegetables according to the packet directions, and chop the spring onion finely. Drain the hot vegetables, and mix with the onion, breadcrumbs and grated cheese. Beat the soy sauce into the egg, and stir them into the stuffing mixture. Fill into the pepper halves. Put the filled peppers, cut side up, on a baking sheet (tray) and place in the oven for 12-15 minutes.

# Cheddared Choice

Cooking time: 10 minutes

| INGREDIENTS | Metric | Imperial | American |
|---|---|---|---|
| *Frozen mixed vegetables* | 600 g | 1¼ lb | 1¼ lb |
| *Large slices of wholemeal (whole wheat) bread* | 4 | 4 | 4 |
| **For the Quick Cheese Sauce** | | | |
| *Dry mustard powder* | ¼ tsp | ¼ tsp | ¼ tsp |
| *Paprika* | ¼ tsp | ¼ tsp | ¼ tsp |
| *Salt* | ¼ tsp | ¼ tsp | ¼ tsp |
| *Wholemeal (whole wheat) flour* | 1 tbsp | 1 tbsp | 1 tbsp |
| *Grated Cheddar cheese* | 4 tbsp | 4 tbsp | 4 tbsp |
| *Water* | 5 tbsp | 5 tbsp | 5 tbsp |
| *Milk* | 2 tbsp | 2 tbsp | 2 tbsp |
| *A few drops of Tabasco* | | | |
| *Lemon juice* | ½ tsp | ½ tsp | ½ tsp |
| *Margarine (see page 13)* | 50 g | 2 oz | ¼ cup |

Cook the frozen vegetables according to the packet directions. While cooking them, cut the crusts off the bread, and toast both sides lightly. Lay the slices close together in a shallow serving dish.

Then make the Quick Cheese Sauce. Mix all the ingredients except the fat in a bowl. Melt the fat in a saucepan. Blend in the ingredients in the bowl, and stir over medium heat until the sauce thickens. Take the pan off the heat.

Drain the vegetables, and spread them evenly on the toast. Pour the cheese sauce over them. Serve at once.

# Chinese Leaf 'Bake'

Cooking time: 20 minutes

| **INGREDIENTS** | Metric | Imperial | American |
|---|---|---|---|
| *Oil for greasing* | | | |
| *(see page 13)* | | | |
| *Medium oatmeal* | *4 tbsp* | *4 tbsp* | *4 tbsp* |
| *Leek (white part)* | *1* | *1* | *1* |
| *Chinese cabbage* | | | |
| *(Chinese leaves)* | *450 g* | *1 lb* | *1 lb* |
| *Low-fat hard* | | | |
| *Cheddar-style* | | | |
| *cheese* | *150-175 g* | *5-6 oz* | *5-6 oz* |
| *Cottage cheese with* | | | |
| *chives* | *113 g* | *4 oz* | *½ cup* |
| *Cumin seeds* | *1 tsp* | *1 tsp* | *1 tsp* |
| *Ground cumin* | *½ tsp* | *½ tsp* | *½ tsp* |
| *Eggs* | *4* | *4* | *4* |
| *Salt and ground* | | | |
| *black pepper* | | | |

Oil the inside of a 20 cm/8 in shallow baking dish suitable for serving. Sprinkle the oatmeal over the base. Set the oven to heat to 190°C/375°F/Gas Mark 5.

Put a large pot of water on to boil. Slice the leek, and shred the greens. Tip them into the pan of water when on the boil, bring back to the boil, then drain thoroughly. Return to the emptied pan.

Shred or grate the hard cheese, and beat into it the cottage cheese, cumin seeds, ground cumin and eggs. (This is best done in a food processor.) Combine the cheese-egg mixture with the vegetables, and season well. Spread the mixture evenly over the oatmeal in the baking dish, and bake for 15 minutes.

# Pasta with Eggs and Wined Mushrooms

Cooking time: 20 minutes

| INGREDIENTS | Metric | Imperial | American |
|---|---|---|---|
| Eggs | 4 | 4 | 4 |
| 'Instant' (4 minute) whole wheat noodles | 225 g | 8 oz | ½ lb |
| Small mushrooms | 450 g | 1 lb | 1 lb |
| Salt | | | |
| Claret or other red wine | 175 ml | 6 fl oz | ¾ cup |
| Margarine (see page 13) | 50 g | 2 oz | ¼ cup |
| Wholemeal (whole wheat) flour | 4 tsp | 4 tsp | 4 tsp |
| Fresh chopped parsley | | | |

Hard-boil (hard-cook) the eggs. Drain them when ready and tap the shells to crack them. While cooking them, also cook the pasta, drain it and keep it warm.

Put the mushrooms in a deep frying pan with 125 ml/4 fl oz/½ cup of the wine and a little salt. Cover and simmer for 3-4 minutes until they are almost tender. Take them out with a slotted spoon, and add the remaining wine and the fat to the pan. Melt the fat, then add the flour and stir until the sauce thickens. Return the mushrooms, mix with the sauce, and leave over the lowest possible heat.

Shell the hot eggs, holding them in a cloth. Cut them in half and pile them in the centre of a warmed flat platter. Spoon the mushrooms and sauce around them in a ring, and edge the mushroom ring with the pasta. Sprinkle this picture-book platter with fresh chopped parsley.

# LIGHT DISHES, SIDE DISHES AND SALADS

## Spiced Bulghar and Onions

Cooking time: 25 minutes      Ⓧ Ⓥ

| INGREDIENTS | Metric | Imperial | American |
|---|---|---|---|
| *Onions* | *225 g* | *8 oz* | *½ lb* |
| *Dried minced garlic* | *¼ tsp* | *¼ tsp* | *¼ tsp* |
| *Oil (see page 13)* | *1 tbsp* | *1 tbsp* | *1 tbsp* |
| *Bulghar* | *75 g* | *3 oz* | *3 oz* |
| *Ground coriander* | *¼ tsp* | *¼ tsp* | *¼ tsp* |
| *Ground cinnamon* | *¼ tsp* | *¼ tsp* | *¼ tsp* |
| *Vegetable stock* | *425 ml* | *¾ pt* | *2 cups (scant)* |

*Salt and ground black pepper*

Chop the onions finely, and sprinkle with garlic. Heat the oil in a saucepan, and sauté the garlicky onions until soft. Off the heat, mix in all the remaining ingredients. Cover the pan and cook gently for 20 minutes or until the stock is all absorbed and the bulghar is soft. Serve with savoury dishes.

### NOTE
If you want to serve the bulghar as a breakfast cereal or as a plain base for a highly flavoured dish or sauce, omit the onions and garlic. Cook the bulghar for 20-25 minutes either in stock or water sharpened with a few drops of Worcestershire sauce.

# Chinese Leaf Chowder

Cooking time: 10 minutes ⓥ

| INGREDIENTS | Metric | Imperial | American |
|---|---|---|---|
| Chinese cabbage (Chinese leaves) | 375 g | 13 oz | 13 oz |
| Vegetable stock from cube | 275 ml | ½ pt | 1¼ cups |
| Onions | 172-225 g | 6-8 oz | 6-8 oz |
| Tomatoes | 175 g | 6 oz | 6 oz |
| Salted peanuts | 50 g | 2 oz | 2 oz |
| Smooth peanut butter | 1 tbsp | 1 tbsp | 1 tbsp |
| Ground white pepper | | | |
| A few grains of chilli powder | | | |

Shred the Chinese leaves finely, especially any stems. Put the stock in a large saucepan, and pack in the leaves. Cover securely. Bring to the boil, and cook for 3 minutes. Draw off the heat. Leave covered.

Finely chop the onions and tomatoes. Crush the peanuts to fragments. Uncover the pan and stir in these ingredients and the peanut butter. Cover and cook over gentle heat for 5 minutes or until the onions are tender. Season with pepper and chilli powder to taste. Serve very hot.

**NOTE**
You can also make the chowder with young spinach leaves or the thinnings of spring leaf vegetables.

# 'Blue' Beans with Poached Eggs

Cooking time: 12 minutes

| INGREDIENTS | Metric | Imperial | American |
|---|---|---|---|
| Eggs *(optional)* | 4 | 4 | 4 |
| Margarine for greasing *(see page 13)* | | | |
| Lettuce leaves | 4 | 4 | 4 |
| Dried sliced onions | 2 tbsp | 2 tbsp | 2 tbsp |
| Lemon juice | | | |
| Frozen sliced green beans from pkt | 454 g | 1 lb | 1 lb |
| Blue Brie-style cheese | 225 g | 8 oz | 8 oz |

If using eggs, prepare an egg poacher or 4 well-greased heatproof bowls standing in simmering water. Break an egg into each greased poacher cup or each bowl, cover and cook gently until set.

While cooking the eggs, shred the lettuce. Put in a saucepan with the onions and a little lemon juice, tip in the still-frozen beans and boiling water as suggested on the packet. Cook according to the packet directions, but without any fat.

Cut or scrape the rind off the cheese and cut the paste into small pieces. Drain the vegetables when ready, and return them to the hot dry pan. Tip in the cheese pieces, and toss or stir for a moment or two until the cheese is half-melted. Spread the mixture evenly over 4 warmed plates and lay a poached egg in the centre of each 'bed' of beans.

Serve with wholemeal (whole wheat) bread and butter.

# Tagliatelle di Napoli

Cooking time: 10 minutes ⓥ

| **INGREDIENTS** | Metric | Imperial | American |
|---|---|---|---|
| *'Instant'* | | | |
| *(4 minute)* | | | |
| *spinach noodles* | *350 g* | *12 oz* | *12 oz* |
| *Salt* | | | |
| *Margarine* | | | |
| *(see page 13)* | *2 tbsp* | *2 tbsp* | *2 tbsp* |
| **For the Tomato-Olive Sauce** | | | |
| *Large Spanish* | | | |
| *onion* | *1* | *1* | *1* |
| *Dried minced garlic* | *1 tsp* | *1 tsp* | *1 tsp* |
| *Fresh tomatoes* | *450 g* | *1 lb* | *1 lb* |
| *Dried basil or* | | | |
| *oregano* | *1 tsp* | *1 tsp* | *1 tsp* |
| *Olive oil* | *2 tbsp* | *2 tbsp* | *2 tbsp* |
| *Dry white wine or* | | | |
| *water* | *2 tbsp* | *2 tbsp* | *2 tbsp* |
| *Salt and ground* | | | |
| *black pepper* | | | |
| *Stuffed olives* | *6* | *6* | *6* |

As a basis, cook the spinach noodles according to
the packet directions. Drain, toss with the fat and
keep warm in a covered serving dish.

For the Tomato-Olive Sauce, chop the onion
finely and sprinkle the garlic over it. Separately,
quarter the tomatoes, squeeze out their seeds, and
chop the flesh. Sprinkle with the dried herbs.
Quarter the olives and keep aside.

In a large heavy frying pan, simmer and stir
the onion and garlic in the oil for 3 minutes. Add
the tomatoes, herbs, and wine or water, and stir
for another 3 minutes. Stir in the olives, season
with salt and black pepper, and pour the sauce
over the pasta.

**NOTE**

For a quite different, more subtle sauce for the
noodles, use the following recipe.

# Almond Cream Sauce

Preparation time: 3 minutes

| INGREDIENTS | Metric | Imperial | American |
|---|---|---|---|
| *Low fat curd or skimmed-milk Quark cheese* | *100 g* | *4 oz* | *½ cup* |
| *Ground almonds* | *100 g* | *4 oz* | *1 cup* |
| *Grated Parmesan cheese* | *25 g* | *1 oz* | *1 oz* |
| *Good pinch each of ground cinnamon and grated nutmeg* | | | |
| *Pouring or half cream (half-and-half)* | *150 ml* | *¼ pt* | *½ cup + 2 tbsp* |
| *Olive oil* | *3 tbsp* | *3 tbsp* | *3 tbsp* |
| *Water* | *2-5 tbsp* | *2-5 tbsp* | *2-5 tbsp* |

Whisk (beat) together or purée in a food
processor all the ingredients except the water.
Add enough water to give the sauce the
consistency you want. Taste and adjust the
flavour before pouring the sauce over the noodles

**NOTE**

If you do not eat dairy foods, use firm tofu (see
page 12) instead of curd or Quark cheese, a good
pinch of ground coriander and a little salt instead
of Parmesan, and silken tofu (page 12) instead of
cream. The sauce will be a little less thick, and a
lot less rich.

# Spinach Strata

Cooking time: 14 minutes                          Ⓥ

| **INGREDIENTS** | Metric | Imperial | American |
|---|---|---|---|
| *Pkt of frozen cut leaf spinach (300 g/10½ oz)* | *2* | *2* | *2* |
| *Dried sliced onions* | *2 tbsp* | *2 tbsp* | *2 tbsp* |
| *Wholemeal (whole wheat) bread slices* | *6-8* | *6-8* | *6-8* |
| *Crunchy peanut butter for spreading and topping* | | | |
| *Salt and ground black pepper* | | | |
| *Grated nutmeg* | | | |
| *Oil (see page 13)* | *1 tbsp* | *1 tbsp* | *1 tbsp* |

Set the oven to heat to 190°C/375°F/Gas Mark 5.
Pour boiling water on the onions in a bowl. Thaw
the spinach according to the packet directions but
with 2 tbsp water instead of any fat. While
thawing, cut the crusts off the bread slices. Put 2
slices aside, and spread the rest with peanut
butter. Use half of them, spread side up, to cover
the base of an oiled, oven-to-table round or
square baking dish; trim them to fit it.

When the spinach is ready, drain it together
with the onions. Season them with salt, pepper
and nutmeg. Spread half evenly in the dish.
Cover with the remaining buttered bread slices,
spread side up, then repeat the spinach layer.
Crumble the reserved bread. Melt 2 tbsp peanut
butter with the 1 tbsp oil, and mix with the
crumbs. Scatter them over the dish. Put in the
oven for 6-8 minutes.

**VARIATION**
You could use 75 g/3 oz grated Cheddar cheese instead of peanut butter. Sprinkle one third over each layer of bread slices, and mix the remaining third with the crumbs.

**NOTES**
The dish can be pre-prepared, and baked when needed at 180°C/350°F/Gas Mark 4 for 15-18 minutes, to heat it through. Otherwise, it takes too long to assemble for a half-hour three-course menu.

# Short-Cooked Leeks

Cooking time: 7 minutes ⓥ

| **INGREDIENTS** | Metric | Imperial | American |
| --- | --- | --- | --- |
| Medium-sized leeks (white and tender green stems) | 4 | 4 | 4 |
| Margarine (see page 13) | 3 tbsp | 3 tbsp | 3 tbsp |
| Water as needed | | | |
| Pinch of ground coriander (optional) | | | |
| Salt and ground black pepper | | | |

Slice the leeks across thinly. Melt the fat in a saucepan, add the sliced leeks and stir over moderate heat for 3 minutes. Add enough water to cover three-quarters of the leeks. Bring to the boil, reduce the heat and cook gently for 4-5 minutes until the leeks are tender. Stir two or three times while cooking. Drain the leeks (keep the cooking liquid for soup), season and turn into a warmed dish.

# Stir-Fried Potato Slices with Sage

Cooking time: 18 minutes                    Ⓥ

| INGREDIENTS | Metric | Imperial | American |
|---|---|---|---|
| Small potatoes | 450 g | 1 lb | 1 lb |
| Shallots | 2 | 2 | 2 |
| OR Spring onions (scallions), bulbs only | 6 | 6 | 6 |
| Oil (see page 13) | 2 tbsp | 2 tbsp | 2 tbsp |
| Cornflour (cornstarch) | 1½ tsp | 1½ tsp | 1½ tsp |
| Pinch of sugar | | | |
| Vegetable stock or water | 225 ml | 8 fl oz | 1 cup |
| Fresh sage leaves, chopped | 2 | 2 | 2 |
| OR Powdered sage | ½ tsp | ½ tsp | ½ tsp |
| Frozen garden peas (optional) | 227 g | 8 oz | 8 oz |
| Tomatoes (optional) | 2 | 2 | 2 |
| Lettuce leaves (optional) | 2 | 2 | 2 |
| Salt and ground black pepper | | | |

Scrub the potatoes, removing any scabbed skin or 'eyes' and cut into 3 mm/⅛ in slices. Slice the shallots or onion bulbs.

Heat the oil in a frying pan with a lid or spatter-proof cover, and stir-fry all the sliced vegetables gently for 5 minutes. Stir in the cornflour and sugar, and cook for 1 minute. Add the stock or water, sage and peas if used, cover and cook gently for 10 minutes. Meanwhile, slice the tomatoes and shred the lettuce leaves if used. Add them to the pan, cover again and cook for 2-3 minutes longer. Season if needed

**NOTE**
Use all the vegetables for a supper dish. For a
side dish of potatoes, omit the peas, tomatoes and
lettuce, and cook the potatoes and shallots alone
for 12 minutes only or until tender.


# Rose-Red Potatoes

Cooking time: 20 minutes                    Ⓧ Ⓥ

| INGREDIENTS | Metric | Imperial | American |
|---|---|---|---|
| *Thin-skinned* | | | |
| *potatoes* | *450 g* | *1 lb* | *1 lb* |
| *Medium-sized* | | | |
| *onion* | *1* | *1* | *1* |
| *Oil (see page 13)* | *3 tbsp* | *3 tbsp* | *3 tbsp* |
| *Can of chopped* | | | |
| *tomatoes in* | | | |
| *tomato juice* | | | |
| *(227 g/ 8 oz)* | *1* | *1* | *1* |
| *Dried savory or* | | | |
| *basil* | *1 tsp* | *1 tsp* | *1 tsp* |
| *Worcestershire* | | | |
| *sauce* | *½ tsp* | *½ tsp* | *½ tsp* |
| *Hot water* | *4 tbsp* | *4 tbsp* | *4 tbsp* |
| *Salt and ground* | | | |
| *black pepper* | | | |

Scrub the potatoes, cut out any scabs, then cut
the potatoes into 1 cm/½ in cubes. Chop the
onion. Heat the oil in a deep frying pan or skillet
with a lid or spatter-proof cover. Add the potato
cubes and onion, and stir over fairly high heat for
4 minutes, until the potatoes begin to brown. Stir
in the tomatoes with their juice. Add the savory
or basil, Worcestershire sauce and 4 tbsp hot
water. Season to taste. Cover the pan, reduce the
heat and cook gently for 10 minutes or until the
potatoes are tender.

# Leeks with Turnip and Apple Sauce

Cooking time: 16 minutes                                  Ⓥ

| INGREDIENTS | Metric | Imperial | American |
|---|---|---|---|
| *Medium-sized leeks* *(white and* *green stems)* | 4 | 4 | 4 |
| *Vegetable stock* | 575 ml | 1 pt | 2½ cups |
| *Young turnips* | 450 g | 1 lb | 1 lb |
| *Sharp eating apples* | 2 | 2 | 2 |
| *Margarine (see* *page 13)* | 1 tbsp | 1 tbsp | 1 tbsp |
| *Pinch of ground* *cinnamon* | | | |
| *Small pinch of* *ground black* *pepper* | | | |
| *A few drops of* *soy sauce* | | | |

Prepare and slice the leeks into 1 cm/½ in rounds. Bring the stock to the boil in a saucepan. Add the leeks, cover, and cook over medium heat for 5 minutes or until the leeks are tender. Drain, and return the stock to the pan. Keep the leeks warm in a covered dish.

While cooking the leeks, top and tail the turnips, and cut them into small chunks. Peel the apples (see note), core them and cut into small pieces. When the leeks are in the dish, add the turnip chunks to the stock, bring back to the boil and cook for 7 minutes. Add the apples, and cook a further 3-4 minutes, until both turnips and apples are soft. Drain, Purée (see note) in a food processor or blender if possible, with the fat and flavouring. Coat the leeks with the sauce. Serve in bowls with oatcakes or bran crispbread.

**NOTE**

In an emergency, omit peeling the apples, and don't purée the turnip and apple chunks. Just toss them with the fat and flavourings, and add them to the leeks.

# Polenta

Cooking time: 25 minutes     Ⓧ Ⓥ

| INGREDIENTS | Metric | Imperial | American |
|---|---|---|---|
| *Warm water* | *275 ml* | *½ pt* | *1¼ cups* |
| *Fine maize meal* | | | |
| *(cornmeal)* | *150 g* | *5 oz* | *1 cup* |
| *Salt* | *¼ tsp* | *¼ tsp* | *¼ tsp* |
| *Hot water* | *700 ml* | *1¼ pt* | *3⅛ cups* |
| *Oil* | *2 tsp* | *2 tsp* | *2 tsp* |

Blend together until quite smooth the warm water, maize meal and salt. Bring the hot water and oil to the boil in a large saucepan. Add the maize meal mixture slowly, stirring constantly to prevent lumps forming. Boil for 2 minutes, still stirring. Reduce the heat, cover the pan and cook very slowly for 15-20 minutes until the water is all absorbed and no gritty taste remains. Turn into a warmed dish.

**NOTE**

Classic polenta is simmered for an hour, but if you use the fine meal, you can get away with this shorter cooking time. This basic cooked grain can be used as a 'bed' for cooked vegetables, or as a breakfast dish like porridge.

If you want to serve it as a side dish instead of rice or potatoes, use vegetable stock instead of water, and omit the salt. If you wish, add 2-3 tbsp dried sliced onions to the cooking liquid with a sprinkling of dried mixed herbs and a pinch of dried minced garlic.

# Brussels Sprouts with Almonds

Cooking time: 9 minutes   ⓥ

| INGREDIENTS | Metric | Imperial | American |
|---|---|---|---|
| *Button mushrooms* | *100 g* | *4 oz* | *4 oz* |
| *Cucumber* | *100 g* | *4 oz* | *4 oz* |
| *Frozen Brussels sprouts* | *454 g* | *1 lb* | *1 lb* |
| *Dried sliced onions* | *2 tbsp* | *2 tbsp* | *2 tbsp* |
| *Margarine (see page 13)* | *1 tbsp* | *1 tbsp* | *1 tbsp* |
| *Flaked almonds* | *3 tbsp* | *3 tbsp* | *3 tbsp* |
| *Lemon juice* | | | |
| *Salt and ground black pepper* | | | |

Put a large pan of water on to boil. Slice the
mushrooms; quarter the cucumber lengthways
and slice it across into 'fans'. When the water
boils, tip in the frozen sprouts and onions. Bring
back to the boil, reduce the heat to fairly low,
and cook the sprouts for 4 minutes. Add the
mushrooms and cucumber and cook for a further
4 minutes. While they cook, melt the fat over low
heat, and stir the almonds into it until one or two
flakes begin to brown. Take the pan off the heat
at once, and turn the almonds on to soft paper.
Drain the vegetables when ready, turn them into
a warmed serving dish and toss with a little lemon
juice, salt and pepper. Add the almonds and any
remaining fat, toss again and serve.

**NOTE**
Take care not to overbrown the almonds.

# Parsley Dumplings

Cooking time: 12 minutes

| INGREDIENTS | Metric | Imperial | American |
|---|---|---|---|
| *Self-raising wholemeal (whole wheat) flour* | *225 g* | *8 oz* | *2 cups* |
| *Shredded vegetarian suet* | *100 g* | *4 oz* | *½ cup* |
| *Fresh chopped parsley* | *2 tbsp* | *2 tbsp* | *2 tbsp* |
| *Good pinch of grated nutmeg* | | | |
| *White pepper* | | | |
| *Beaten eggs* | *2* | *2* | *2* |
| *Vegetable stock if needed* | | | |

Put a large pan of water on to boil. Mix all the ingredients for the dumplings thoroughly, adding the eggs last to bind the mixture; if necessary add a little stock to make a firm dough. On a floured surface, pat the dough into a block 2.5 cm/1 in thick, and cut it into 30-32 cubes (this is quicker than rolling it into balls). Drop the cubes, a few at a time, into the boiling water, and cook for 5 minutes or until they rise and dance on the surface, and are tender and swollen. Remove with a slotted spoon at once, to make room for more cubes, and drain on a tilted plate.

**NOTES**
Taste one of the first batch of dumplings to make sure it is fully cooked.

You could serve the dumplings as a light supper dish if sprinkled well with grated cheese. Serve with a green salad.

# Curried Salad, Hot or Cold

Cooking time: 17 minutes

| **INGREDIENTS** | Metric | Imperial | American |
|---|---|---|---|
| *Medium-sized carrots* | 2 | 2 | 2 |
| *Large radishes* | 6 | 6 | 6 |
| *Small green pepper* | 1 | 1 | 1 |
| *Spring onions (scallions), green and white parts* | 6 | 6 | 6 |
| *8 cm/3 in piece cucumber* | 1 | 1 | 1 |
| *Sharp eating apple* | 1 | 1 | 1 |
| *Vegetable stock* | 275 ml | ½ pt | 1¼ cups |
| *Tomato juice* | 50 ml | 2 fl oz | ¼ cup |
| *Curry powder* | ¼-½ tsp | ¼-½ tsp | ¼-½ cup |
| *Canned flageolet or green lima beans, drained* | 125 g | 4 oz | ½ cup |
| *Chilled cottage cheese or yoghurt (see note)* | 6 tbsp | 6 tbsp | 6 tbsp |

Chop the carrots coarsely. Slice the radishes thickly. De-seed the pepper and cut the flesh into 1 cm/½ in squares. Cut the spring onions into 1 cm/½ in pieces, and the cucumber and cored apple into 1 cm/½ in cubes; do not peel them.

Heat the vegetable stock and tomato juice in a saucepan. Add the carrot, radishes and pepper at simmering point, sprinkle with ¼ tsp curry powder, bring to a slow boil, and cook, covered, for 5 minutes. Add the spring onions, reduce the heat slightly and simmer, covered, for another 5 minutes. Add the beans, cucumber and apple and cook, uncovered, for 4 minutes. If the sauce is still quite thin, raise the heat and boil for 1-2 minutes to reduce it. Taste and stir in a little extra curry powder if you wish. Serve hot at once, topping each helping with a spoonful of cottage cheese; or cool, and serve cold topped with yoghurt.

**NOTE**
If you want to avoid dairy foods, you could use whisked Tofu Dressing (page 70) instead of cottage cheese or yoghurt.

# Palermo Cabbage

Cooking time: 12 minutes ⓥ

| INGREDIENTS | Metric | Imperial | American |
|---|---|---|---|
| *Firm-hearted green cabbage* | *450 g* | *1 lb* | *1 lb* |
| *Margarine (see page 13)* | *3 tbsp* | *3 tbsp* | *3 tbsp* |
| *Clear honey* | *1 tbsp* | *1 tbsp* | *1 tbsp* |
| *Lemon juice* | *1 tbsp* | *1 tbsp* | *1 tbsp* |
| *Salt and ground black pepper* | | | |
| *Water* | *4 tbsp* | *4 tbsp* | *4 tbsp* |
| *Fresh tomatoes* | *275 g* | *10 oz* | *10 oz* |

Shred the cabbage, removing any core and hard ribs. Melt the fat in a saucepan, and toss the cabbage in it over medium heat for 1 minute. Stir in the honey, lemon juice, a little seasoning and 4 tbsp water. Reduce the heat, cover the pan and simmer for 5 minutes. Quarter the tomatoes, stir them in and cook for a further 5 minutes. Stir round once more while cooking. Serve with any juices in the pan.

# Buttered Greens

Cooking time: 8-10 minutes

| **INGREDIENTS** | Metric | Imperial | American |
|---|---|---|---|
| *Small heads of spring greens (collards)* | *450 g* | *1 lb* | *1 lb* |
| *Boiling water* | | | |
| *Butter or margarine (see page 13)* | *2 tbsp* | *2 tbsp* | *2 tbsp* |
| *Oil (see page 13)* | *2 tbsp* | *2 tbsp* | *2 tbsp* |
| *A few grains each of salt, ground black pepper, grated nutmeg and brown sugar* | | | |

Wash the vegetables thoroughly, and trim off any
stems. Bring 2.5 cm/1 in depth of water to the
boil in a deep frying pan or pot-roaster which
holds the heads side by side. Add the greens and
1 tbsp of the fat. With two wooden spoons, turn
the greens over in the water for 2-3 minutes until
the leaves soften (wilt). Cover the pan with a lid
or spatter-proof cover, reduce the heat, and
simmer for 5-7 minutes until the heads are
tender. Drain, then press out excess moisture by
squeezing the heads in a cloth. Split them
lengthways. Heat the oil, remaining fat and
seasonings in the dry pan, return the greens and
turn them over until well coated. Serve at once.

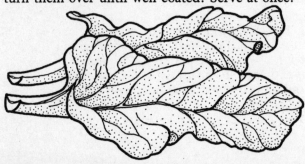

# Short-Cooked Celery and Carrots

Cooking time: 12 minutes

| **INGREDIENTS** | Metric | Imperial | American |
|---|---|---|---|
| *Hot vegetable stock* | | | |
| *(see method)* | *150 ml* | *¼ pt* | *½ cup + 2 tbsp* |
| *Dried sliced onions* | *2 tbsp* | *2 tbsp* | *2 tbsp* |
| *Young celery stalks* | *225 g* | *8 oz* | *8 oz* |
| *Medium-sized* | | | |
| *carrots* | *2* | *2* | *2* |
| *Margarine (see* | | | |
| *page 13)* | *1 tbsp* | *1 tbsp* | *1 tbsp* |
| *Oil (see page 13)* | *2 tbsp* | *2 tbsp* | *2 tbsp* |
| *Oregano* | *½ tsp* | *½ tsp* | *½ tsp* |
| *Natural yoghurt* | | | |
| *(optional)* | *150 ml* | *¼ pt* | *½ cup + 2 tbsp* |

Crumble a vegetable stock cube into the hot water
in a jug. Add the dried sliced onions. Slice the
celery and carrots. Heat the fat and oil in a
saucepan, and sauté the celery and carrots for 2
minutes. Strain the stock, and add 150 ml/
¼ pt/½ cup + 2 tbsp to the saucepan with the
onions. Add the oregano. Half-cover the pan, and
cook gently for 8 minutes. The celery should be
almost tender. Uncover, and cook for 3-4 minutes
longer, until the vegetables are tender and the
liquid is almost absorbed. Stir in the yoghurt if
you use it, and let the dish stand beside the stove
until needed.

Serve with pasta, or with egg dishes.

# Broccoli with Hazelnut Sauce

Cooking time: 10 minutes                                    (V)

| **INGREDIENTS** | Metric | Imperial | American |
|---|---|---|---|
| *Pkt of frozen broccoli spears (454 g/1 lb)* | *1* | *1* | *1* |
| *Vegetable stock* | *275 ml* | *½ pt* | *1¼ cups* |
| *Ground hazelnuts (see method)* | *125 g* | *4 oz* | *1 cup* |
| *Pinch of salt* | | | |
| *Margarine (see page 13)* | *2 tsp* | *2 tsp* | *2 tsp* |
| *Dry white vermouth* | *2 tsp* | *2 tsp* | *2 tsp* |

Cook the broccoli spears in the stock as the
packet instructions direct. Turn the hazelnuts into
a bowl (they are available ready-ground from most
good Health Food stores); mix in the salt, and dot
with the fat.

Drain the broccoli when ready, reserving the
stock. Turn the broccoli into a warmed serving
dish, and cover while you make the sauce. Mix
the vermouth with the nuts, and stir in enough
hot stock to make a thick sauce of the consistency
you want; the hot liquid should melt the fat. Pour
the sauce over the broccoli.

**NOTE**
For a main dish, you could add plainly boiled
pasta to the broccoli, and pour the sauce over
both. Alternatively, you could grill (broil) halved
tomatoes while cooking the broccoli, and add
them to the dish.

# Cucumber and Walnut Salad

Preparation time: 8 minutes (V)

| **INGREDIENTS** | Metric | Imperial | American |
|---|---|---|---|
| *Cucumbers* | *450 g* | *1 lb* | *1 lb* |
| *Radishes* | *8* | *8* | *8* |
| *Large green* | | | |
| *  pepper* | *1* | *1* | *1* |
| *Spring onion* | | | |
| *  (scallion), green* | | | |
| *  and white parts* | *1* | *1* | *1* |
| *Walnut pieces* | *50 g* | *2 oz* | *2 oz* |
| *Leaves of 1 sprig* | | | |
| *  fresh thyme* | | | |
| *OR Dried thyme* | *¼ tsp* | *¼ tsp* | *¼ tsp* |
| *Chopped parsley* | | | |
| *  (optional)* | | | |
| **For the Soy Dressing** | | | |
| *Soy sauce* | *2 tbsp* | *2 tbsp* | *2 tbsp* |
| *Oil (see page 13)* | *1½ tsp* | *1½ tsp* | *1½ tsp* |
| *Lemon juice* | *1½ tsp* | *1½ tsp* | *1½ tsp* |
| *Ground ginger* | *¼ tsp* | *¼ tsp* | *¼ tsp* |
| *Clear honey* | *2 tsp* | *2 tsp* | *2 tsp* |

Put the ingredients into your salad bowl as you prepare them. Halve the cucumbers lengthways, and slice them across into thin half-moons. Slice the radishes, discarding the ends. Halve and core the pepper, removing most of the seeds (leave a few for their 'bite'). Chop the pepper, spring onion and walnut pieces together coarsely, and add them to the bowl with the herbs. Mix all the dressing ingredients in a jug.

At the table, toss the salad with about half the dressing. (This dressing keeps for weeks. Make extra, chill it, and use it later to make a sliced raw mushroom salad or for marinating tofu (see page 26).

# Quick Potato and Mushroom Salad

Cooking time: 5 minutes                                      Ⓥ

| **INGREDIENTS** | Metric | Imperial | American |
|---|---|---|---|
| *Can of new potatoes in salt water (580 g)* | *1* | *1* | *1* |
| *Button mushrooms (optional)* | *4-6* | *4-6* | *5-6* |
| *Dill seeds or cumin seeds* | *1 tbsp* | *1 tbsp* | *1 tbsp* |
| **For the French Dressing** (see note) | | | |
| *French mustard* | *1 tsp* | *1 tsp* | *1 tsp* |
| *Salt* | *½ tsp* | *½ tsp* | *½ tsp* |
| *White pepper* | *¼ tsp* | *¼ tsp* | *¼ tsp* |
| *Pinch of white sugar* | | | |
| *White vinegar or lemon juice or 1 tbsp of each* | *2 tbsp* | *2 tbsp* | *2 tbsp* |
| *Olive oil* | *4 tbsp* | *4 tbsp* | *4 tbsp* |

Make the dressing first if not made ahead (it stores well in an airtight jar or bottle if refrigerated). To make it, blend the flavourings together in a jar with an airtight lid or stopper. Stir in the oil, little by little; close and shake the jar after each addition. Lastly, add the vinegar and/or lemon juice, close the jar and shake thoroughly to blend it in. Shake again just before use.

Strictly, a potato or pulse salad should be dressed just after the ingredients have been cooked so that they cool in the dressing. You certainly have not got time to cook and cool your potatoes in half an hour. The following compromise is tasty, and it is less rich than most bought potato salads.

Drain the canned potatoes, and halve them if large. Slice the mushrooms if you use them. Put both in a bowl and sprinkle with the seeds. Heat the dressing to boiling point in a saucepan, and pour it over the vegetables. Toss well, then turn into a chilled salad bowl, and refrigerate. The dressing should cool in a few minutes.

**NOTE**
You could use commercially-bottled French Dressing in an emergency (see page 16).

# Carrot and Olive Salad

Preparation time: 8 minutes          Ⓥ

| INGREDIENTS | Metric | Imperial | American |
|---|---|---|---|
| Young carrots | 450 g | 1 lb | 1 lb |
| Stuffed olives | 16-20 | 16-20 | 16-20 |
| Orange juice (from carton or home-pressed) | 3 tbsp | 3 tbsp | 3 tbsp |
| Lemon juice | 1 tbsp | 1 tbsp | 1 tbsp |
| Tofu dressing (see overleaf) | 150 ml | ¼ pt | ½ cup + 2 tbsp |
| Chopped parsley (optional) | | | |

Grate the carrots coarsely, using an electric appliance if possible. Turn into a bowl. Chop the olives coarsely, and add them. Toss with the orange and lemon juice. Mix in the tofu dressing with a fork, blending it in thoroughly. Pile the salad in a dish. If you have time, garnish with chopped parsley.

# Tofu Dressing

Preparation time: 5 minutes     Ⓥ

| INGREDIENTS | Metric | Imperial | American |
|---|---|---|---|
| Silken tofu | 275 ml | 1/2 pt | 1 1/4 cups |
| Soy dressing | | | |
| (page 67) | 2 tsp | 2 tsp | 2 tsp |

Whisk (or purée in a blender) the tofu with 2 tsp Soy Dressing. For a spicier dressing, add more Soy Dressing.

You only need half this quantity of dressing for the Carrot and Olive Salad, but it is not worth making less. It keeps well in a refrigerator. Use the rest to dress a coleslaw.

# Mixed Pulse Salad

Preparation time: 4 minutes

| INGREDIENTS | Metric | Imperial | American |
|---|---|---|---|
| Can of chickpeas | | | |
| (garbanzos) | | | |
| (400 g/14 oz) | 1 | 1 | 1 |
| Can of red kidney | | | |
| beans (425 g/15 | | | |
| oz) | 1 | 1 | 1 |
| Can of sweetcorn | | | |
| (198 g/7 oz) | 1 | 1 | 1 |
| French Dressing, | | | |
| home-made | | | |
| (page 68) or | | | |
| bottled | 3 tbsp | 3 tbsp | 3 tbsp |
| Chopped parsley | 1 tbsp | 1 tbsp | 1 tbsp |

Drain all the cans. Jumble the chickpeas, beans and corn in a salad bowl. Just before serving, toss with the dressing, coating well, and mix in the parsley.

70

# Leaf Salad with Tofu

Preparation time: 6 minutes      Ⓥ

| INGREDIENTS | Metric | Imperial | American |
|---|---|---|---|
| *Small head of firm-hearted round (iceberg) lettuce or Chinese cabbage* | ½ | ½ | ½ |
| *Fresh or dried thyme* | ¼ tsp | ¼ tsp | ¼ tsp |
| *Button mushrooms* | 100 g | 4 oz | 4 oz |
| *French Dressing, home-made or bottled* | 50 ml | 2 fl oz | ¼ cup |
| *Marinated tofu (page 26)–see note* | 175 g | 6 oz | 6 oz |
| *Chopped fresh chives or parsley* | 2 tsp | 2 tsp | 2 tsp |

Shred the lettuce and mix with the thyme in your salad bowl. Slice the mushrooms thinly, and toss with the dressing in a small bowl. Drain the tofu, cut it into small cubes, and place on a plate with the chives or parsley beside them.

At serving point, toss the mushrooms and dressing lightly with the lettuce. Fold in the tofu cubes carefully, without breaking them if possible. Sprinkle with some or all of the chopped chives or parsley, depending on the width of your bowl.

**NOTE**
Half a standard block of tofu slit horizontally weighs about 175 g/6 oz when marinated.

# Cabbage-Pineapple Slaw

Preparation time: 6 minutes

| **INGREDIENTS** | Metric | Imperial | American |
|---|---|---|---|
| *Firm white or* | | | |
| *Savoy cabbage* | *450 g* | *1 lb* | *1 lb* |
| *Green spring* | | | |
| *onions* | | | |
| *(scallions)* | | | |
| *(leaves only)* | *5-6* | *5-6* | *5-6* |
| *Can of pineapple* | | | |
| *in natural juice* | | | |
| *(227 g/8 oz)* | *1* | *1* | *1* |
| *Seedless raisins* | *75 g* | *3 oz* | *½ cup* |
| **For the Dressing** | | | |
| *Natural yoghurt* | *150 ml* | *¼ pt* | *½ cup +* |
| *AND* | | | *2 tbsp* |
| *Low-calorie* | | | |
| *mayonnaise* | *2 tbsp* | *2 tbsp* | *2 tbsp* |
| *OR Tofu Dressing* | | | |
| *(page 70)* | | | |

Cut out the cabbage core, and shred the leaves
with the spring onion tops. (If desperate for time,
do it in a food processor). Drain the pineapple,
and cut the fruit into small pieces if needed.
(keep the juice to drink). Add the pineapple and
raisins to the cabbage. Mix the mayonnaise into
the yoghurt if using them. Then blend the salad
with either prepared dressing.

# SNACKS AND STARTERS

A snack may be anything from an outsize 'burger' to a few olives served with drinks. Hungry teenagers and midnight guzzlers usually want hearty snacks such as stoutly-filled sandwiches, pie or a wedge of pizza. An office worker's desk-top lunch is likely to be much the same.

Sandwiches, plain or toasted, are the quickest and most convenient kind of healthful packed or snack meal to prepare from 'scratch'. Vegetarian 'burgers or hot dogs can be made in half an hour using a packet mix, but they are usually fried so they are rich in fat. Pies and pizzas can be made ahead or bought and stored, but lack the vital zing of fresh salad ingredients. Wholemeal (whole wheat) bread sandwiches or salad-filled pitta breads are a better choice on both scores.

Your only problem may be to find enough suitable fillings. Commercially-made vegetarian spreads are pricey (except for fat-loaded processed cheese spreads). Cottage cheese is not exciting as a daily diet base, and the distinctive taste of peanut butter soon palls. It really needs fresh-flavoured 'extras'. But unless very simple, two- or three-layer fillings take valuable time to prepare when you are working at speed, apart from the clutter you have to assemble and wash up.

It is a good idea, therefore, to make ahead a few quick spreads of your own to vary your choice; they don't take long, and can be kept chilled for a day or two or frozen as a 'backstop' if you allow for slow thawing overnight.

One of the merits of such fillings is that they also make easy dinner-time 'starters'. They can be served like a pâté, filled into small, hollowed tomatoes, or spread on toast fingers and arranged in a 'star' pattern on small plates. This way, they can also be served with drinks.

When you are trying to get a speedy meal together, do not attempt, however, to make snacks such as canapés to serve with drinks before dinner. A bowl of olives, bought rice crackers or nuts and raisins is quite enough. Concentrate on getting the meal on the table.

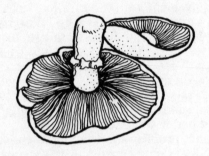

# Made-Ahead Spreads

Any of the following spreads can be used in sandwiches or as a filling for hollowed tomatoes or cucumber 'cups'. They are best made in an electric blender. Otherwise, mince (grind) and sieve the ingredients to make them smooth.

**TO SERVE AS A STARTER**
Place a small mound of any stiff spread on each of four small plates, garnish with parsley sprigs and serve with hot toast.

Alternatively, put two or three soft spreads into small bowls, and offer as a choice of spreads with toast fingers or crackers.

# Red Lentil Pâté

Cooking time: 20 minutes

| INGREDIENTS | Metric | Imperial | American |
|---|---|---|---|
| Red lentils | 225 g | 8 oz | 8 oz |
| Low fat Cheddar-style cheese | 50 g | 2 oz | 2 oz |
| Soft wholemeal (whole wheat) breadcrumbs | 50 g | 2 oz | 2 oz |
| Margarine (see page 13) | 50 g | 2 oz | 2 oz |
| Few drops of lemon juice | | | |
| Pinch of cayenne pepper | | | |
| Pinch of ground cumin | | | |
| Salt and ground black pepper | | | |
| Vegetable fat, melted | | | |

Boil the lentils until soft. Cool them slightly, then process them with the cheese, breadcrumbs and margarine. Work in a few drops of lemon juice, a pinch each of cayenne pepper and ground cumin, and a little salt and pepper. Taste to get the flavour you want. Pack the pâté into a bowl or small loaf tin, level the top and run a little melted vegetable fat over the top to prevent it drying out. Use within 48 hours or freeze.

**NOTE**
For a yellow-golden pâté, use yellow split peas instead of lentils.

# Bean Spread

Preparation time: 5 minutes

| INGREDIENTS | Metric | Imperial | American |
|---|---|---|---|
| Cooked haricot beans | 125 g | 4 oz | 4 oz |
| OR Can of haricot beans 213 g/ 7½ oz | 1 | 1 | 1 |
| Natural yoghurt or silken tofu | 3 tbsp | 3 tbsp | 3 tbsp |
| Worcestershire sauce | | | |

Drain the cooked haricot beans or can of beans. Grind or process them with the yoghurt or tofu and flavour to taste with a little Worcestershire sauce.

**NOTE**
Do not freeze if made with yoghurt.


# Green Pea Spread

Preparation time: 5 minutes

| INGREDIENTS | Metric | Imperial | American |
|---|---|---|---|
| Cooked fresh or thawed frozen garden peas | 225 g | 8 oz | 8 oz |
| Low fat smooth curd cheese | 50 g | 2 oz | 2 oz |
| Pinch of grated nutmeg | | | |
| Salt and ground black pepper | | | |

For this attractive vivid spread, process the peas with the curd cheese, nutmeg and a little salt and pepper.

# Aubergine (Eggplant) Spread

Cooking time: 10 minutes

| INGREDIENTS | Metric | Imperial | American |
|---|---|---|---|
| Aubergine (eggplant) | 350 g | 12 oz | 12 oz |
| Ground almonds | 50 g | 2 oz | 2 oz |
| Low fat smooth curd cheese or silken tofu | 225 g | 8 oz | 8 oz |
| Pinch of mixed spice if using tofu | | | |
| Lemon juice | 1 tbsp | 1 tbsp | 1 tbsp |
| Few drops of onion juice | | | |

Halve the aubergine lengthways. Grill it, skin side up, until the flesh is soft. Strip off the skin, and chop the flesh into a bowl. Then process it with the ground almonds, curd cheese or tofu and a pinch of mixed spice. Work in the lemon juice and a few drops of onion juice. Put in a pot, cover and chill. Use within 48 hours.

# Toast Canapés

Preparation time: 6 minutes (for 12 canapés)

**FOR SNACKS**
Buy ready-made small toasts. If you cannot get
whole-grain ones, don't worry; you will not use
enough to matter, diet-wise. (Two or three types
are sold in most city supermarkets, and they store
perfectly in an airtight container.)

Cover the toasts with your chosen spread
neatly, peaking it in the centre. If you have time,
sprinkle the spread with finely chopped parsley,
sieved hard-boiled egg yolk or a sprinkling of
paprika, depending on the spread's colour and
flavour.

**FOR STARTERS**
Arrange 3 or 4 small round or square canapés in a
clover-leaf pattern on each of four small plates.
Offer with small paper napkins.

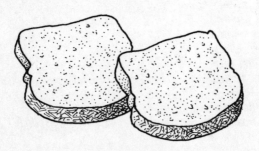

# Quick 'C' Sandwiches

Here are a few simple sandwich ideas to top up
your daily input of vital vitamins and minerals
with spreads that you can buy. The quantities
given are for 1 sandwich, made with slices from a
large wholemeal (whole wheat) loaf.

## PEANUT BUTTER-ORANGE SANDWICH
Spread one slice of bread with peanut butter. Cover it with 2 or 4 thin slices of peeled orange, cut across the segments. Sprinkle very lightly with ground black pepper. Cover with a second slice of bread spread with margarine (see page 13).

## CHEESE-ORANGE SANDWICH
Make a sandwich as above but use thinly sliced mozzarella cheese instead of peanut butter.

## COTTAGE-GRAPEFRUIT SANDWICH
Spread two slices of bread with cottage cheese with chives. Cover one slice with two grapefruit slices cut like the orange above, then into small bits. Top with the second slice of bread.

## TOMATO-CHEESE SANDWICH
Spread two slices of bread with low-fat smooth curd cheese. Sprinkle one with a little grated onion. Cover with 3 or 4 pieces of tomato flesh without the seeds and juice. Grind a little black pepper over them. Top with the second slice of bread.

## 'FRUIT SALAD' SANDWICH
Spread one slice of bread with cottage cheese with pineapple. Cover it with orange slices cut as above. Top with a second slice of bread spread with coarse-cut orange marmalade (for its fibre value).

## CHRISTMAS SANDWICH
Spread two slices of bread thinly with margarine (see page 13). Spread one with a vegetarian mincemeat (obtainable from Health Food stores). Top with the second bread slice.

# Toasted Snack Sandwiches

Cooking time: 3 minutes      Ⓥ

| INGREDIENTS | Metric | Imperial | American |
|---|---|---|---|
| *Wheatgerm (enriched) or high-bran bread slices without crusts* | *12* | *12* | *12* |
| *Large tomatoes* | *2* | *2* | *2* |
| *Margarine (see page 13) for spreading* | | | |
| *Green Pea Spread (page 76)* | *6 tbsp* | *6 tbsp* | *6 tbsp* |
| *Peanut butter* | *6 tbsp* | *6 tbsp* | *6 tbsp* |
| *Wooden toothpicks* | *12* | *12* | *12* |

Use a small tin (oblong) loaf. Slice the tomatoes into 4 rounds each, discarding the ends. Spread 8 slices of bread with margarine. Then cover the spread sides of 4 slices with Green Pea Spread, using 1½ tbsp on each. Cover with the second bread slice, fat side up. Lay 2 tomato rounds on each slice. Spread the last 4 (uncovered) bread slices with peanut butter. Place them, buttered side *down*, on the tomato. Press lightly with your palm to 'seal' the sandwiches. Set the grill (broiler) to heat, then cut each sandwich into 3 equal strips or fingers, and stick a toothpick through each, to hold the bread slices together. Place the strips, cut side down, on a sheet of foil. Toast under the grill (broiler) for 1–2 minutes on each side until lightly coloured. Serve 3 strips per person while still warm.

**VARIATION**
You could use low-fat soft cheese with herbs or chives instead of Green Pea Spread.

# Leek and Apple Packets

Cooking time: 6 minutes

| INGREDIENTS | Metric | Imperial | American |
|---|---|---|---|
| *White part of leek* | *100 g* | *4 oz* | *4 oz* |
| *Vegetable stock* | *150 ml* | *¼ pt* | *½ cup + 2 tbsp* |
| *Eating apple, unpeeled* | *100 g* | *4 oz* | *4 oz* |
| *Radishes (optional)* | *2* | *2* | *2* |
| *Lettuce leaves (from round medium-sized lettuce)* | *2* | *2* | *2* |
| *Natural cottage cheese* | *3 tbsp* | *3 tbsp* | *3 tbsp* |
| *Salt to taste* | | | |
| *Whole wheat pitta breads* | *2* | *2* | *2* |

Slice the leek across, and cook it in the stock until tender. Drain (use the stock for soup). Cool the leek while you core and chop the apple, chop the radishes if used, and shred the lettuce leaves finely. Mix all these ingredients with the cheese. Warm the pitta breads, cut them in half across and fill with the salad and cheese mixture. Use for a packed meal or snack, or for brunch.

# About Formal Starters

When you're trying to make a three-course meal, go for a starter with few ingredients, if possible ones which you keep on the shelf or have ready-prepared. Keep hard-boiled (hard-cooked) eggs in the refrigerator, for instance, if you eat eggs. They keep well for a week or more, and dress up any cold dish beautifully. A 50-g/2-oz dollop of cottage cheese mixed with a few capers or chopped stuffed olives makes a presentable starter if served on a lettuce leaf with sliced egg or crumbled yolk around or over it.

Quartered hard-boiled (hard-cooked) eggs themselves make a good starter if 'bound' with low-calorie mayonnaise (see page 14); sprinkle a vivid garnish of red paprika on top.

An almost 'instant' starter is a wedge of melon per person, served with a small bowl of ground ginger and a grinder of black pepper. A small portion of a simple salad such as sliced tomatoes sprinkled with French Dressing (page 68) is also a good choice. In both cases, make sure that the same fruit or salad vegetable does not feature in the rest of your meal.
Tomato-sauced noodles after Tomato Salad would be a bad idea.

Below, there are a few examples of other quick fruit and vegetable starters, and a richer egg dish for a special occasion or for when you serve a low-fat meal.

# Tomato or Cucumber Cups

Cut medium-large tomatoes in half across, or cut unpeeled thick cucumbers into 6 cm/2¼ in lengths, discarding the ends. Make sure that they stand on end level. With a teaspoon, scoop out the tomato seeds and juice or take out the cucumber seeds and some of the flesh from one end without piercing the other. You will then have hollow cups. Turn them upside-down to drain for a few minutes. Then season the insides with a few drops of soy sauce. Fill with your chosen spread, mounding it high; if possible, choose a contrast-coloured spread such as Green Pea Spread in Tomato Cups or Red Lentil Pâté in Cucumber Cups. Garnish each cup (if you have time) with a parsley sprig or with a dab of soft cheese.

To serve as a starter, place 2 or 3 tomato halves or cucumber cups on each of 4 small plates. Serve with small knives and forks.

# Tomato and Avocado Salad

Preparation time: 7 minutes ⓥ

| INGREDIENTS | Metric | Imperial | American |
|---|---|---|---|
| Lettuce leaves | 4 | 4 | 4 |
| Can of whole plum tomatoes (397 g/14 oz) | 1 | 1 | 1 |
| Ground black pepper | | | |
| French dressing, home-made (see page 68) or bottled | 6 tbsp | 6 tbsp | 6 tbsp |
| Lemon juice | 2 tbsp | 2 tbsp | 2 tbsp |
| Firm ripe avocado pears | 2 | 2 | 2 |

Tear up the lettuce and divide the bits between 4 small bowls. Drain the tomatoes over a jug (keep the juice to drink). Divide the tomatoes between the bowls, halving them if large. Sprinkle with pepper. Mix the (well shaken) dressing and lemon juice in a bowl. Halve the avocados, take out the stones, and scoop out the flesh in pieces with a spoon. Toss the pieces at once in the dressing, and spoon the fruit and dressing over the tomatoes.

# Grapefruit Cocktail

Preparation time: 4 minutes                                    Ⓥ

| **INGREDIENTS** | Metric | Imperial | American |
|---|---|---|---|
| *Cans of grapefruit segments in natural juice 285 g/10 oz)* | *3* | *3* | *3* |
| *Sherry* | *2 tbsp* | *2 tbsp* | *2 tbsp* |
| *Ground ginger* | | | |

Drain the fruit (keep the juice to drink). Divide
the segments between 4 stemmed dessert glasses.
Sprinkle with sherry. Serve with a small bowl of
ground ginger.

**Variation**
For a fancier starter, fill drained grapefruit
segments into avocado pears, halved lengthways,
stoned and brushed with sherry on the cut sides.
You will only need 2 cans of fruit for 2 pears.

# Happy Apple Starter

Preparation time: 6 minutes

| **INGREDIENTS** | Metric | Imperial | American |
|---|---|---|---|
| *Red-skinned dessert apple* | *1* | *1* | *1* |
| *Piece of cucumber* | *50 g* | *2 oz* | *2 oz* |
| *Dry white wine* | *2 tbsp* | *2 tbsp* | *2 tbsp* |
| *Cooked fresh or thawed, frozen (uncooked) small green peas* | *100 g* | *4 oz* | *4 oz* |
| *Dried savory* | *1 tsp* | *1 tsp* | *1 tsp* |
| *Salt and ground black pepper* | | | |

84

Core and chop the apple into dice-sized pieces
with the (unpeeled) cucumber; if you use a food
processor, use the pulse setting to avoid chopping
them too small. Toss well with the wine, to coat
all the apple. Mix in the peas and savory. Season
if you wish. Pile in a salad bowl, then spoon into
small bowls or dessert glasses at the table. Serve
with wholemeal (whole wheat) crackers.

# Eggs in Curry 'Cream' Sauce

Preparation time: 7 minutes

| **INGREDIENTS** | Metric | Imperial | American |
| --- | --- | --- | --- |
| *Large lettuce or Chinese cabbage leaves* | *4* | *4* | *4* |
| *Capers, drained* | *2 tsp* | *2 tsp* | *2 tsp* |
| *Hard-boiled (hard-cooked) eggs* | *6* | *6* | *6* |
| *Low-calorie mayonnaise* | *50 ml* | *2 fl oz* | *¼ cup* |
| *Silken tofu* | *5 tbsp* | *5 tbsp* | *5 tbsp* |
| *Curry powder* | *¼-½ tsp* | *¼-½ tsp* | *¼-½ tsp* |
| *Lemon juice* | | | |

Place the leaves flat on 4 small plates. Sprinkle
with a few capers. Shell the eggs, cut them in half
across, and arrange 3 egg halves in the centre of
each lettuce leaf.

For the Curry 'Cream' Sauce, whisk (beat)
together the mayonnaise, tofu, ¼ tsp curry
powder and a few drops of lemon juice until
smooth. Taste, and add extra curry powder or
lemon juice if you wish. Spoon some of the
mixture over each egg half.

Serve with pumperknickel or quartered
wholemeal (whole wheat) pitta breads.

# SWEET THOUGHTS

## Dessert Ideas

Most conventional desserts are easy to adapt to
vegetarian meals. Agar-agar can be used instead of
gelatine, for instance. If you do not use dairy
foods, there are subtitutes in Health Food stores
for milk, butter and cream if you want desserts
based on them. However, if you have read what
modern experts say about eating for health, you
have probably given up high-cholesterol custards
and soufflés, creamy mousses and fatty fritters
anyway, plus syrupy canned fruits.

You may be tempted to revert though, when
scrambling to make half-hour meals because those
canned fruits, along with instant whips,
cream-lathered tarts and bought iced gâteaux do
provide time-free fancy desserts.

Although fresh fruit is the best dessert of all,
health-wise and taste-wise, there are certain
occasions when more is required than just a plain
apple, orange or banana or stewed fruit with
muesli (see pages 24-5).

Here, then are a few more showy ideas for
the (moderately!) health-conscious, which take
only a few moments to prepare.

## Winter Delight

Preparation time: 5 minutes                    Ⓥ

| INGREDIENTS | Metric | Imperial | American |
|---|---|---|---|
| *Sweet whole wheat or oatmeal biscuit (crisp cookie) crumbs (see notes)* | *125 g* | *4 oz* | *4 oz* |

|                                              |        |        |        |
|----------------------------------------------|--------|--------|--------|
| *Can of peach slices in fruit juice (285 g/10 oz)* | *1*    | *1*    | *1*    |
| *Sugarless fruit spread (see page 15)*       | *4 tbsp* | *4 tbsp* | *4 tbsp* |

Place 1 heaped tbsp biscuit (cookie) crumbs in
each of 4 dessert glasses. Drain the fruit, halve or
chop the slices into pieces, and divide them
between the glasses. Cover with the remaining
crumbs, and top each helping with a spoonful of
fruit spread.

**NOTES**
There are a good many different kinds of
whole-wheat and oatmeal biscuits (cookies) on the
market. Choose, if you can, a type which contains
bran and is made with unrefined brown sugar or
molasses.

Biscuit (cookie) crumbs keep well in an
airtight jar, so they can be prepared ahead and
stored for a week or more.

**VARIATION**
For a more sophisticated dessert, reserve the fruit
juice, and purée the fruit. Mix the purée with 50
g/2 oz ground almonds to make a paste, adding a
few drops of lemon juice and enough of the fruit's
own juice to make it spreadable and creamy.
Spoon this fruit 'cream' over the crumbs in the
bottoms of the glasses, then cover with crumbs
and top with spread as above. This version takes
about 10 minutes to prepare.

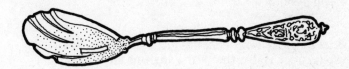

# Eastern Dream

Preparation time: 6 minutes

| INGREDIENTS | Metric | Imperial | American |
|---|---|---|---|
| Preserved dessert dates | 12 | 12 | 12 |
| Bananas (about 275 g/10 oz) | 2 | 2 | 2 |
| Can of pineapple in natural juice (227 g/8 oz) | 1 | 1 | 1 |

Stone the dates, chopping them if it speeds up the job. Put them in a dessert bowl. Peel and slice the bananas, and mix the slices with the dates. Open the can of pineapple, chop any large pieces of fruit, and mix both fruit and juice with the dates and bananas, coating the bananas thoroughly with juice.

# Gourmet Pears

Preparation time: 6 minutes

| INGREDIENTS | Metric | Imperial | American |
|---|---|---|---|
| Full fat soft smooth cheese | 50 g | 2 oz | 1/4 cup |
| Cottage cheese with pineapple | 50 g | 2 oz | 1/4 cup |
| Sherry | 2 tbsp | 2 tbsp | 2 tbsp |
| Seedless raisins | 25 g | 1 oz | 1 oz |
| Medium-sized dessert pears | 2 | 2 | 2 |

Beat together both cheeses and the sherry. Stir in the raisins. Halve the pears, dig out any cores with a teaspoon, and brush all over with a little

extra sherry. Arrange on a platter, cut side up.
Spoon the cheese mixture on top. Sprinkle with a
few flaked almonds. Chill (while you eat the main
course).

**VARIATION**
For a non-alcoholic dessert, make Gourmet
Pineapple by changing the fruit to canned
pineapple rings. Use a 227 g/8 oz can of pineapple
rings in natural juice. Open and drain the can
before mixing the cheeses, and use the juice
instead of sherry.

# Spiced Honey Toasts

Cooking time: 4 minutes

| INGREDIENTS | Metric | Imperial | American |
|---|---|---|---|
| Large square slices of wholemeal (whole wheat) bread | 4 | 4 | 4 |
| Margarine (see page 13) | | | |
| Large banana | 1 | 1 | 1 |
| Clear honey | 5 tbsp | 5 tbsp | 5 tbsp |
| Water | 2 tbsp | 2 tbsp | 2 tbsp |
| Ground cinnamon | 1/4 tsp | 1/4 tsp | 1/4 tsp |
| Ground ginger | 1/8 tsp | 1/8 tsp | 1/8 tsp |
| Pinch of ground black pepper | | | |
| Pine nut kernels | 2 tbsp | 2 tbsp | 2 tbsp |

Toast the bread lightly on both sides. Cut off the
crusts, and spread fat on one side; lay on warmed
plates, spread side up. Skin and slice the banana,
and lay the slices on the toasts. Melt the honey,
water and spices in a saucepan, and pour it over
the banana slices. Sprinkle with the nuts. Serve
hot, with knives and forks.

# Sparkling Peaches

Preparation time: 5 minutes

| INGREDIENTS | Metric | Imperial | American |
|---|---|---|---|
| *Fresh peaches* | 2 | 2 | 2 |
| *Low fat smooth soft cheese or cold brown rice* | *4 tbsp* | *4 tbsp* | *4 tbsp* |
| *Sugar or sugarless sweetener (see page 14)* | | | |
| *Sparkling white wine, chilled* | | | |

Dip the peaches in boiling water, skin and halve
them. Remove the stones. Mix a little sugar or
sweetener into the cheese or rice. Place 1 tbsp
cheese or rice in the bottom of each of 4 large
stemmed wine glasses. Place a peach half,
hollowed side down, on each spoonful of cheese
or rice. At serving point, pour enough sparkling
wine into each glass to come level with the top of
the fruit.

**NOTE**
Make this dessert during the meal, just after the
main course. No one will mind waiting a few
moments for it at that stage. If you skin the
peaches earlier, they will discolour.

**VARIATION**
As an alternative which you can make ahead (but
which takes a few minutes longer), you could
serve Rosy Peaches. Drain a 300 g/11 oz can of
strawberries in natural juice, and mash the fruit
to a purée with a little of the juice. (Do not use
raspberries because they need sieving.) Sweeten
the purée to taste, then spoon it over the peaches
instead of wine.

# MAKING A 30-MINUTE MENU

Rapid meal-making may be your daily lot; if so, you will probably just use this book for new quick dishes to try. Sometimes, however, every cook has to scramble a meal together because of a social emergency. Your husband may bring the boss home, your daughter and boy friend want a quick meal before a show, or there's an unexpected club meeting you simply must go to. You'll cope – but to save chaos in the kitchen, you'll be wise to have a ground-plan for dealing with sudden demands, just in case ........

The first step is to pick two or three full dinner menus which will adapt easily to different occasions, say by adding extra pasta for hungry teenagers or vivid garnishing for guests. There are some sample menus below using recipes from this book, but you can use your own favourites if you prefer, or mix them. Try to choose menus which fit together just as well as if you have all the time in the world to make them. The starter course should have different ingredients and lighter ones from the main course, and be a different texture and colour. So should the dessert. Choose your main courses first, picking ones which do not need much preparation. Some recipes in this book are only suitable for two-course meals if you only have about 30 minutes unless you have a ready-made starter to hand.

Having picked your menus, try them out to see if you like what you have chosen, and how long they take to make. Warning! You will probably not get a full-scale, three-course meal on the table in half an hour at your first attempt when following new recipes. They always take longer to make than ones which you know well. When you are making several new dishes at the same time, the odds against your beating the clock first time round are even longer. But one merit of your trial run is that you will spot short cuts to take and see how you can dovetail your various tasks next time. For instance, any recipe which can be left to 'cook' itself once in the pot or oven, is marked (X); if you prepare it first you will be free to cope with others which may need more attention.

You'll notice at once that the cooking time given at the head of each recipe means just that; it is not practical to include the time it takes to prepare and combine the ingredients because cooks work at different rates, depending on their skill and on their tools. Your chances of making a meal in about 30 minutes are vastly improved if you have a food processor and blender, for instance, because you can do 'instant' chopping, shredding, grating and puréeing; a blender makes finer purées and vegetable sauces than a processor, although it may be too powerful for coarse chopping and reduce tender foods to mush.

An important point to remember (if you are not a routine quick meal-maker) is that emergencies seldom announce their coming ahead of time. Once you have made your menu choices, make sure that you *always* keep *all* the ingredients in stock, either on the shelf or in the refrigerator or freezer (if they quick-thaw). Their keeping capacity is one reason why a good many canned and frozen ingredients have been used in this book's recipes (the other being that they are ready-prepared and partly cooked for you).

Do not rely only on knowing that you have these ingredients to hand. Know exactly where they are. When the countdown comes, you will not have time to search along your shelves or through the freezer's contents. You must be able to lay hands on everything you need without a pause. You will save a lot of time too if you assemble everything, open cans and undo packages before you start work.

Even when you have advance warning, you will still be wise to use canned and frozen products if the alternative is to prepare fresh foods hours ahead of time. Frozen green beans cooked 'from frozen' are certainly better for you than fresh beans sliced before you go to the office and left in a pan of water until the evening. Remember that when frozen vegetables are suggested in the recipes, the thawing and cooking times given are for commercially frozen, packeted vegetables. If you use home-frozen vegetables, you may have to adjust the cooking times to suit them.

Besides the ingredients for your special menu, keep a few staple quick-cooking stand-bys in stock. 'Instant' (four minute) pasta, for instance, is an excellent helper-out. Although small shapes of conventional pasta cook quickly, the merit of the 'instant' kind is that you do not have to watch it. Once you have poured boiling water over the strands, you can forget the whole thing until you are ready to drain and use it; and it can 'double' either as a side dish or as a basis of a ten-minute main dish with a sauce or thawed vegetable.

Feel flexible about sauces. Some non-starchy ones can be stored frozen. Most sauces can be made several hours ahead and left ready to reheat. Often, you can swap one sauce for another if it is quicker or more convenient to make – or you can simply forget about making a sauce at all, and sprinkle your pasta, rice or vegetables with melted fat and a few chopped, dried herbs, sesame seeds or chopped nuts.

Do not get carried away into making bigger changes to your menu than this especially once you start cooking. Simplify your chosen dishes if it helps you, by leaving out a sauce or altering a spice, but don't change one dish for another unless, of course, you happen to have a ready-made substitute in the fridge. On the whole, once your mind is racing, thinking ahead as you deal with each process in turn, don't break the pattern. In only half an hour or so you haven't got time to think out a new one, let alone act on it.

If you can lay your hands on your ingredients and tools in one sweep before you start work, and have all your actions planned, you should have no trouble in putting a tasty supper or brunch on the table in half an hour; any main-course or light dish in this book is suitable. Presenting a three-course dinner in around that time is going to demand quick thinking and nimble fingers. Still, if you are spry and deft, and stick to a practised menu, it can be done.

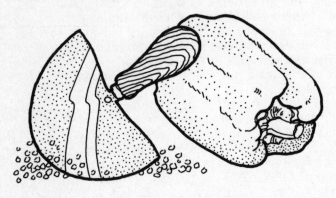

# THREE-COURSE DINNER MENUS

These menus are designed for four people.

1. Happy Apple Starter (page 84)
   Record-Quick 'Ratatouille' (page 32)
   Winter Delight (page 86)

2. Tomato Cups (page 82)
   Curried Potato Garland (page 30)
   Eastern Dream (page 88)

3. Quick Potato and Mushroom Salad
   (page 68)
   Spectrum Stir-Fry (page 31)
   and
   'Instant' Pasta (page 21)
   Sparkling Peaches (page 90)
   – made during the meal

4. Grapefruit Cocktail (page 84)
   Stuffed Cabbage Leaves (page 33)
   and
   Reheated Brown Rice (page 22)
   Spiced Honey Toasts (page 89)

# INDEX OF RECIPES